*The Contemporary Composers*

Series Editor: Nicholas Snowman

# HARRISON BIRTWISTLE

*Michael Hall*

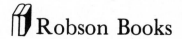

Robson Books

*Acknowledgements*

My thanks to those who helped me with this book: to Brenda Townsend who led me through it, David Lumsdaine who provided background, John Woolrich who lent me his doctoral thesis, Eric Forder who lent me scores, Universal Edition who permitted me to reproduce them, Marian Robertson and Mary Timbrell who typed and typed and typed, and, not least, to Harry himself.

FIRST PUBLISHED IN GREAT BRITAIN IN 1984 BY ROBSON BOOKS LTD., BOLSOVER HOUSE, 5-6 CLIPSTONE STREET, LONDON W1P 7EB. COPYRIGHT © 1984 MICHAEL HALL

**British Library Cataloguing in Publication Data**
Hall, Michael
 Harrison Birtwistle.—(Contemporary composers: 4)
 1. Birtwistle, Harrison
 I. Title    II. Series
 780′.92′4    ML410.B

 ISBN 0-85051-270-3

MU
R

# CONTENTS

soloist and chorus 40–1; journeying through verse one to find verse two 41–44; bending organum with the use of adjacencies 44–5; the canons of verse six 46; the dénouement 46–8

The foundation of the Pierrot Players 49–50; external referents — parody 50–2; internal referents — ego and collective unconscious 52–3; inner speech 53–4; interlocking techniques 55–6; psychological, social and spiritual allegory 56; *Punch and Judy* as a 'source' opera 57–8; relationship between protagonist and chorus in Greek tragedy 58–9; the problem of abstractness in allegory 59–60; the influence of Schenkerianism 60–1; the interlocking allegories in *Punch and Judy* 62–7; the introspective protagonist 67–8

The Orpheus legend in opera 69–71; the difficulties in completing *The Mask of Orpheus* 72–3; new concepts of time 73–4; time and spatial distance in music 74–5; the three temporal dimensions of *Nenia* 75–7; 'for better or for worse' 77–8; Euridice as image of the divine mystery 78–80; the three layers of the composers' evolutionary process 80–2; logical and infra-logical groupings 83; time triumphant counter-balanced by time transcended 84–6

Objective and subjective time in *La Plage* 87–9; constructing an aria from random numbers 89–92; on spaces in progress 92–4; the use of the three geometries in music 95; self as a construct 96–7; the invention of a fragment of monody and the proliferations surrounding it by means of a 'dance of numbers' 98–103

'Pulse and drone and simple harmonies' 104–5; the elemental, mysterious quality of pulse 105–6; bells

# EDITOR'S PREFACE

It is no secret that our epoch favours a museological rather than a prospective approach to musical activity. Such a situation is, of course, the reflection of a cultural climate, but it is also the result of problems particular to the evolution of musical language during this century.

Whatever the fundamental causes, the effects are clear. The repertoire of 'classical' music has been extended backwards in time and enlarged with the inclusion of many important works as well as a great number of lesser ones. At the same time the 'standard' works of the eighteenth and nineteenth centuries have become more than ever entrenched in a musical world very largely conditioned by market considerations and thus inimical to contemporary endeavour. One cannot blame record company employees, concert promoters and artists' agents for being more interested in quick turnover than in the culture of their time. The results are inevitable: re-recordings of the same symphonies and operas multiply; performances of the same 'early' music, claiming to be less inauthentic than their rivals, abound; and conductors' careers are made with an ever-diminishing bunch of scores.

Where does this leave the music written yesterday and today? The answer is not encouraging. As far as western Europe and the United States are concerned, contemporary works inhabit a number of well defined ghettos.

In West Germany it is the radio stations that commission and perform new scores and, naturally enough, their concern is to satisfy their specialist listeners rather than to cultivate a wider public. Except for a certain number of important but brief 'shop

1

window' festivals, contemporary music is hardly a living affair.

In the United States composers find sanctuary in the universities—comfort and security but little contact with the general musical public outside the walls, whilst symphony orchestras, reliant for their existence on the whims of the rich and generally conservative, tend to play safe.

In the UK, outside the BBC and one or two imaginative enterprises, the situation is depressing—on the one hand inadequate state funds spread too thinly, on the other, excellent but hungry orchestras competing for the same marketable fodder. Indeed, at the moment there is not even a modest but representative contemporary music festival worthy of inter-national attention.

France, with its rigorous but narrow education system giving little place to the non-literary arts, has suddenly in these last few years woken up to the charms of music and begun to invest more and more heavily in this new passion. Yet is spite of all the talk and activity, contemporary music outside Paris attracts small audiences; the work of 'decentralisation' so dear to Gallic politicians is more arduous here than in other countries.

This is not the place for a thorough survey of the status of contemporary music in the world in general. However, it seems clear that even a brief glance at a few different countries reveals the existence of an uneasy relationship between the contemporary public and its music. Certainly, a few independently minded and cultivated musicians seek by their artistic policies to persuade the musical public to accept the endeavours of the present as well as the rich and varied musical traditions and structures of the past.

This new series of books, each introducing a different living composer, seeks to supplement the work of the pathfinders. The scope of the series does not reflect any particular musical 'party line' or aesthetic; its aims are to be representative of what exists, and to supply the listener who stumbles across a new piece at a Prom or on record with the essential facts about its composer—his life, background and work.

NICHOLAS SNOWMAN

# 1:  1934-57

BIRTWISTLE SAYS THAT TO be any good a composer must go to extremes. He must be positive; he must project ideas with such boldness and clarity no one could possibly mistake his meaning. This is what so impressed him about Boulez and Stockhausen when he first heard *Le marteau sans maître* and *Zeitmasse* in 1957. For years new music has been beset by technical considerations, but these pieces 'released us from that. You really knew what they were getting at. They were crucial pieces. They were visions'.

It was this encounter which led to *Refrains and Choruses* (1)\*, his first acknowledged work, the piece which ended five years of doubt and hesitation. He wrote it, he says, off the top of his head. No technical fetters hindered him nor had he any premeditated plans other than a simple organizing principle and the implications of the words of the title. All his attention was devoted to what needed to be said. Caution about 'the sound of the language' was thrown to the winds. In the end he produced something so uncompromising and of such conviction that it was bound to make an impact.

Since then, as well as a film score for Sidney Lumet and incidental music for plays at the National Theatre, where he is Director of Music, he has composed about sixty pieces ranging

---

\* Numbers in brackets refer to the order in which works appear in the Catalogue on pp. 154-72, where more information can be found.

from short instrumental works to two operas—*Punch and Judy* (18) and *The Mask of Orpheus* (60). There are no songs, sonatas, quartets, concertos or symphonies among them, none of the abstract forms which have dominated music since the eighteenth century. Nor are there any of the equally abstract 'process' titles other contemporary composers adopt. When not referring to a text he is setting, the titles of his pieces suggest an older, less sophisticated tradition: *Monody for Corpus Christi, Entr'actes, Chorales, Tragoedia, Verses, Eight Lessons for Keyboards.*

Perhaps the explanation lies in his background. He was born on 15 July 1934 in the Lancashire mill-town of Accrington, which is situated between the larger towns of Blackburn and Burnley, some 20 miles north of Manchester. It too is uncompromising. No foliage softens the stark hills which enclose it; nothing disguises the fact that its function is purely industrial. There is only row upon row of workers' cottages, and above them, dominating them, the tall chimneys of the mills and the high arches of the railway viaduct (an image Birtwistle uses in his second act of *The Mask of Orpheus* when Orpheus descends to Hades!)

He is the only child of parents who ran a smallholding on the edge of the town. He was therefore somewhat isolated and apart, and this may explain why, on his own admission, he has always felt an outsider. He now finds it incongruous, for instance, that he should be considered a member of the musical establishment when he feels so estranged from it. A quiet, rather secretive person, he tends to keep himself to himself. He avoids company, preferring the intimacy of his family and a few friends. But if he rarely attends public events such as concerts, he can frequently be found in art galleries. He is probably in an art gallery at this moment, gazing at the Cézannes. Should you meet him, you would get the impression of someone utterly self-possessed. He seems invulnerable to the external environment, yet he has the air of a countryman about him. His manner is stolid and unflappable, his Lancastrian voice soft-grained, his appearance a little unkempt. When he was actively involved with the National Theatre he divided his time between his house in Twickenham and a remote cottage on the Hebridean island of

4

Raasay, but now his position as Associate Director, Music is much more advisory than executive and there is more time for composing, he lives in even remoter surroundings—a converted farmhouse near Rocamadour in southwest France.

When he recalls his childhood, he remembers with particular affection his mother. It was she who encouraged his music. Although he never became a keyboard player, through her he was able to tinker on the organ of the local Methodist church from time to time. And it was she who bought him a clarinet when he was seven and arranged for him to have lessons with the local bandmaster. Accrington is one of those unusual towns in the North where the band is not brass, but military—that is, it includes woodwind instruments. Eventually, Birtwistle became good enough to be a member, and it was there that he received his musical education. The repertoire consisted of marches, hymns, competition pieces and selections from the shows. Every year he would also play in the orchestra which accompanied the local operatic society's production of a Gilbert and Sullivan opera, and the local choral society's performance of *The Messiah*.

Birtwistle claims that composing began as soon as the clarinet had been put into his hands. He describes his early pieces as 'sub Vaughan Williams'. During the war, and indeed until about 1952 when Birtwistle went to the Royal Manchester College of Music, the musical environment in Britain, certainly as far as new music was concerned, was parochial in the extreme. Throughout his formative years, Birtwistle's idea of the modern would be nothing more advanced than the *Fantasia on a Theme by Tallis*, which he would have heard on the wireless. In contrast to what he would be playing in the band, its modality would have been startlingly unusual. It is no wonder that when he eventually found himself as a composer his style was strongly biased towards modes, and also towards that form of music Vaughan Williams so often favoured, the processional.

Birtwistle may remember with pleasure the music of his childhood, but he recalls with absolute loathing the schools he attended. He describes them as 'the fag-end of the industrial revolution'. The regimentation, the bullying, the beatings, the learning by rote, the total lack of sympathy for anything but

5

school-work and games, and above all 'those dreadful lessons in class singing'—all these were anathema to him. As a result, he became a persistent truant. His only refuge was music, and it was music which finally released him from the torment when in 1952 he won a scholarship to study at the Royal Manchester College of Music.

His teachers there included Frederick Thurston for clarinet and Richard Hall for composition. Hall was rare among composition teachers at that time. He was one of the very few who actually encouraged his pupils to be adventurous and compose in that daring 12-note style! But if this was a boon, Birtwistle's real teachers, certainly as far as composition was concerned, were his peers. Here he was exceptionally lucky for among them were some of the most talented musicians of his, or indeed any other, generation. They were all catalysts to each other. The 'ideas' man was Alexander Goehr, who had a cosmopolitan background, and who always kept in contact with what was happening on the continent, particularly at Darmstadt, the mecca of the avant-garde. Peter Maxwell Davies, with whom Birtwistle was particularly friendly, studied at Manchester University as well as at the College, and had deep interests in medieval and Indian music. John Ogdon and Elgar Howarth were outstanding instrumentalists. Together they formed the New Music Manchester Group in 1953 and gave concerts of music which could not be heard elsewhere—mainly 12-note or serial pieces, but rarely those of the Darmstadt School.

The highlight of the Group's activities actually took place when most of them had left Manchester in January 1956. It was then that they gave their one and only London concert. The programme, however, was representative of the music they had been presenting in the North. It consisted of new works by Maxwell Davies and Goehr, and pieces by Elizabeth Lutyens, Webern, Richard Hall, Elmer Seidel and Skalkottas.

Birtwistle's name, it will be noted, is not on this list. At Manchester, where the prevailing style was serial music, nothing he composed satisfied him. Whenever he tried his hand at a twelve-note piece his efforts came to nothing. His energy,

6

therefore, was devoted to discovering what did satisfy him, and this proved a long, difficult task. Early on, however, he encountered the music of Satie. He was particularly attracted to the three *Gymnopédies*, in which each piece seems to be going through the same music from a different angle. It was as if he were looking at facets of a diamond. In an instant, he realized that he preferred the circling immobility of Satie's style to what he was to call the 'goal-orientated' music of the classical and romantic traditions. Satie seemed to belong to an older, more mysterious, more universal way of doing things. Later Birtwistle came to realize that the analogy with diamonds was very similar to a view held by Varèse, and although Birtwistle has never consciously imitated Varèse, the parallels between them are very strong, as many critics have since observed. Both composers have a primeval almost elemental quality about them.

The event which made the deepest impression on him during his student days, however, was the performance, under Goehr's father, Walter Goehr, of the *Turangalîla Symphony* by Messiaen, which took place at the BBC in 1954. Here, he discovered, was a way of creating new-sounding music without recourse to serialism. He was impressed by the mysterious ambivalence of the piece, by the stark contrast between the monumental and the blatantly sensuous, by the cyclic construction, and, as with Satie, by the fact that Messiaen organized his music not to move progressively forward in a straight line, but to go from static block to static block almost without heed of destination.

Not even this event, however, released the constraints on him. He still found it impossible to compose. The following year he completed his course at Manchester and joined the band of the Royal Artillery for his National Service. Fortunately he was stationed near London, and so was able to keep abreast of what was happening in contemporary music. After the two statutory years, he went to the Royal Academy for a year to continue his clarinet studies, this time with Reginald Kell. In May 1957 he encountered *Le marteau sans maître* and *Zeitmasse*; in August Maxwell Davies's *Alma Redemptoris Mater*, the first of his pieces to use medieval techniques, was performed at Dartington Summer School. Birtwistle was not present at the performance, but shortly afterwards the floodgates opened. By New Year's Eve *Refrains and Choruses* was complete.

At that time, the main difficulty confronting most young composers in Britain, and not just Birtwistle, was the problem of continuity. Although it was generally agreed that a fresh start ought to be made in music, nobody wanted to go the whole hog and reject the past utterly, as had happened on the continent, particularly in Darmstadt—the immediate past, yes; the whole of the past, no. Continuity was actually the issue at stake. Young British composers wanted, somehow, to find a way between the 'goal-orientated' structures of classical composers and their successors, and the fragmentary, almost completely static style of their Darmstadt colleagues, who were claiming that in discovering pointillism, the single note, they had virtually abandoned logical continuity altogether.

In a nutshell, what the British composer wanted was the ethos of the new music, its iconoclasm, its lack of referential associations, anecdotes or propaganda, while at the same time preserving a continuity which had a measure of discernible logic about it. Goehr led the way in his *Fantasia for Orchestra*, Op. 4, which was given at the 1956 Darmstadt Summer School. On the one hand, it was consistently athematic, on the other, each note in his series was held as a pedal at one stage, so that a kind of *cantus firmus* was produced. Then the following year came Davies's *Alma Redemptoris Mater*. Here the *cantus firmus* is not held in long pedal notes, but is integrated into the general texture as the *cantus firmus* in the tenor parts of the *ars nova* had been. The important fact was that both composers had written pieces based on a continuous line. 'All we had needed,' one wag put it, 'was a washing-line upon which to hang things.' In the years that followed, all talk in composing circles was of single lines, how to construct, expand and proliferate them.

The ideas had particular interest for Birtwistle because, as a clarinet player, he instinctively thought in terms of a single line. All his music, no matter how dense it might be, is a single line filled out by other lines moving in parallel motion with it, or by heterophony, the presentation of differing versions of the same line simultaneously. This melodic, as opposed to harmonic, style relates him not only to medieval music, but also to Vaughan Williams, Satie, and such oriental traditions as Indonesian Gamelan and Japanese Gagaku.

Concerning the construction of the single lines, or 'monodies' as Birtwistle prefers to call them, there were three options open to him. One was a continuous, through-composed structure such as the antiphon Maxwell Davies used in *Alma Redemptoris Mater*. Here the line is perpetually in a state of development and consequently contains no literal repetitions. The other two were sectionalized structures in which repetitions are inherent. The first was the binary or ternary structure of the typical folk song; the second the self-repeating isorhythmic tenor of the *ars nova*. Since the first option would be too goal-orientated and the second too formal and too closed, Birtwistle chose the third.

Isorhythm involves the superimposition of a self-repeating rhythmic pattern of a certain length (*talea*) upon a self-repeating melodic pattern of a different length (*color*) so that the beginnings of the two patterns only coincide once in a while. In this example, taken from Albert Seay's *Music in the Medieval World\**, the *color* is six notes long, the *talea* five.

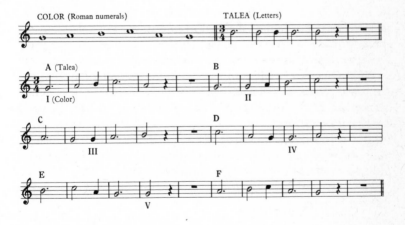

* Albert Seay, *Music in the Medieval World* (Prentice-Hall, 1975), p. 133.

The cycle is completed when the *color* is repeated five times and the *talea* six. This is a textbook example; actual practice was usually more elaborate. In Machaut's instrumental motet *Hoquetus David* (30), which Birtwistle arranged for the Pierrot Players in 1969, the cycle consists of a 12-note *talea* repeated eight times and a 32-note *color* repeated thrice. However, some of the cycles Birtwistle himself invented can go in the opposite direction and be very short. His *talea* may consist of two, his *color* of only three notes. This is the length of the cycle of *Verses* for clarinet and piano (15), which will be considered in detail in Chapter three.

Isorhythm has considerable advantages for Birtwistle. The most obvious is that it need not have either beginning or end—it is therefore the very antithesis of goal-orientation. In *Hoquetus David* the cycle is particularly long, and when it is completed Machaut changes the pattern in order to herald closure. However, as the textbook example suggests, the inherent quality of isorhythm is that the process could continue *ad infinitum*. Another advantage is that interesting material can be obtained automatically. All the composer need do is devise a *color* and *talea*: the rest follows without further effort.

Birtwistle's other composing maxim can now be stated. The first is 'go to extremes'; the second is 'preserve decision-making only for high level matters'. Composition, he says, is concerned with taking decisions, but if a composer has to take decisions about everything that happens in music he will seize up and rapidly come to a halt. This was the situation he had experienced in Manchester. To circumvent the problem a composer must find ways and means of allowing music to write itself. All he should concern himself with are important issues. The most appropriate analogy would be from the world of computers. Let the composer write the programme, but let automatic processes, such as isorhythm, do the routine work for him.

Turn to the score of *Refrains and Choruses*, however, and it will be difficult to find any evidence of isorhythm, at least in the medieval sense. The horn rhythm at the opening may be the *talea*, the clarinet line which follows the *color*, but neither of these patterns is repeated mechanically, indeed there are no repetitions anywhere in the piece. It gives the impression of being entirely through-composed. It resembles, in fact, a Beethovenian structure in that at the start there is a rhythmic followed by a melodic motif (the notes C B D flat) both of which develop, reach a climax a little over two-thirds through, then wither and ultimately die. Those who are fairly familiar with Birtwistle's music will know that the melodic motif of a falling semitone and a rising tone begins nearly all of his pieces. It is the basic seed from which all things grow.

Organic growth is of crucial importance to him. For years his favourite bedside book was D'Arcy Thompson's *On Growth and Form*, the classic work on how things develop and the shapes they take.* His home is full of strange flora and fauna he has collected over the years. Stones, skulls, flower paintings by Philip Sutton are but a few. Growth and form, of course, depend upon the responsiveness of the organism to the restrictions put upon it, or the advantages offered to it, by the surrounding world, the soil, the weather. The same seed will produce different results in different circumstances. So too will the same musical seed. *Refrains and Choruses* is poles apart from *The Fields of Sorrow*, but both start with the same motif. Later, Birtwistle was to find a rhythmic seed as well: the iambic throb of the heart-beat. He thus enhances the impression that the process is akin to something living. Yet things that live must die. They have a destiny; they are goal-orientated. In opting for organic growth Birtwistle has brought back the situation he intended to abandon, perpetual recurrence has been combined with a process which is circumscribed and unique.

This paradox, however, is the very core of Birtwistle. It constitutes what must be called his central organizing principle. An article Meirion Bowen contributed to *British Music Now*† began:

---

* D'Arcy Thompson, On Growth and Form, abridged edition (*Cambridge University Press*, 1961).
† Lewis Foreman (ed.), *British Music Now* (Elek, 1975), p. 60.

11

Everything about Harrison Birtwistle bespeaks a son of the soil. Pay him a visit at his Twickenham home, and you are likely (at least in summer) to find him curled up asleep like a hedgehog in a corner of the garden, covered in leaves and bits of grass. Prod him with conversation on any subject, and he is by turns docile and prickly: he digresses easily from music and other professional matters to talk of trees, birds and insects, which absorb him just as much . . . but he could, in fact, be described as a hedgehog in another, entirely different sense—that popularised by Sir Isaiah Berlin in his famous essay on Tolstoy, which takes its starting-point from a fragment of Archilochus: The fox knows many things, but the hedgehog knows one big thing.

In *The Hedgehog and the Fox*, Sir Isaiah characterizes hedgehogs as those

> who relate everything to a single, central vision, one system less or more coherent or articulate, in terms of which they understand, think and feel—a single, universal, organizing principle in terms of which alone all that they are and say has significance.*

Birtwistle is the first to admit these attributes and confirms them when he says that he has the impression he has composed the same piece over and over again. In fact, he takes monism to extreme lengths. Every aspect of his mature work stems from the central vision and there are no deviations. Once the organizing principle has been grasped, all follows inevitably. One small illustration of it is that, unlike Maxwell Davies (a veritable fox), he does not borrow his monody from plainsong in *Refrains and Choruses* but invents his own. Since his thought is centripetal rather than centrifugal, he prefers internal rather than external models or points of reference. He borrows liberally from himself but not from others. When he does (as in *Medusa* (31), where a Bach chorale-prelude is first parodied then mutilated) the piece is usually withdrawn.

---

* Isaiah Berlin, *Russian Thinkers* (Hogarth Press, 1978), p. 22.

The central organizing principle comes out of the two maxims and can be stated thus: start with an absolutely regular and uniform pattern of the simplest, most predictable kind then superimpose upon it a pattern which is its extreme opposite—something capricious and unpredictable. Invert this statement, express it more succinctly, and another way of putting it would be: base everything on a combination of chance and necessity. This will doubtless be familiar to everyone for it is nothing else than the combination which governs the growth, development and evolution of all living things. Biochemists tell us that organic life results from purely accidental and unpredictable events perpetuated by the necessity of chemical reactions. In this context the word 'necessity' means a condition, principle or conclusion that cannot be otherwise, in other words something absolutely regular and predictable. Birtwistle's position is paradoxical only in so far as the very principle of life is paradoxical.

Isorhythm is one example of a necessary condition. There are many others in Birtwistle. The capricious, accidental and unpredictable patterns he employs also come from a number of sources. Since *Refrains and Choruses* was composed off the top of his head, the disruptions which throw things into disorder derive from his fantasy, his own capriciousness. Others are the result of mistakes or, in one case, a printing error. In the last of the seven sections the chorus is a five-note chord, which at first is widespread but then gradually contracts into a cluster. On one appearance there is a glaring mistake in the flute part. Far from being distressed, he is actually delighted with this. The consistency of his pattern has been deliciously flawed by something he did not calculate.

The most interesting disruptions, however, are those which happen automatically. One is known technically as an essential accident or uncertainty. It occurs when two totally independent chains of events coincide. A meteor on one trajectory accidentally coincides with a meteor on another trajectory. The result is absolutely necessary and therefore essential. Isorhythm is an essential uncertainty. *Color* and *talea* are two totally independent chains of events which converge to produce unexpected and therefore always interesting results. Most of Birtwistle's scores abound in such accidents.

Equally pervasive is his use of operational accidents or uncertainties. These are most familiar in games of chance—dice and roulette for instance. Their outcome is uncertain because of the practical impossibility of governing the throw of the dice or the spinning of the ball with sufficient precision. In a sense, from Birtwistle's point of view, these are the most attractive of all because no human interference is involved, no decisions whatsoever need be taken. Since the late 1960s, when an old school-friend working at Imperial College supplied him with sheet upon sheet of random numbers thrown up by a computer, this kind of accident has been his mainstay. In fact, the random numbers are the 'secret formula' friends and colleagues have been whispering about for years. Birtwistle guards them with spines bristling!

During the course of this book we shall have ample opportunity to discuss his central organizing principle in detail, but for the moment let us consider one aspect of *Refrains and Choruses* which exposes it most clearly: the scoring of the piece. Out of this Birtwistle creates the drama. It is for wind quintet: flute, oboe, clarinet, horn and bassoon—a homogeneous group, uniform and regular in that certain properties are constant throughout. One member, however, is an odd-man-out—the horn, the only brass instrument in the group. Since the central organizing principle requires that something uniform and regular be set off by something capricious, then capriciousness is the role the horn must play. Were the ensemble a string quartet, the cello, the only instrument held between the knees, would have this role. The horn is therefore the protagonist and the drama the conflict between capricious individuality and the solidarity of the group. Since most drama starts with action from the protagonist, *Refrains and Choruses* begins with the horn announcing the *talea*, the dynamic format through which the action will unfold. Gradually the horn's capriciousness becomes more and more assertive until, in the sixth section, it becomes almost uncontrollably headstrong. The *peripeteia*, or turning point, comes when (at the climax of the piece) the other instruments acting as a united chorus virtually silence the horn. Roles have been exchanged. In that moment the chorus plays the assertive part. Thereafter the horn becomes absorbed into the chorus and the drama is over.

It is a familiar, indeed a standard, formula which Birtwistle uses over and over again. One also finds it in plays by Aeschylus or Sophocles, except that dramatists such as these would express the conflict according to the conventions of Greek tragedy, that is to say, more obliquely. The protagonist would offend the forces of cohesive order inadvertently. Nevertheless, *Refrains and Choruses* reflects Birtwistle's abiding passion for Greek theatre and poetry. It was almost certainly the lure of writing music for a production of *The Oresteia* which clinched his decision to join The National Theatre in 1974. His interest, however, is not intellectual—he knows little of Greek history or philosophy—it has more to do with sensuality. Again it involves extremes. In his opinion, no other culture has expressed the tension between the individual and society so vividly. At the moment he is contemplating setting poems by Palladas, which his friend Tony Harrison has translated.* Palladas (*c*. AD 319–391) is often called the last poet of Greek paganism. 'His are the last hopeless blasts of the old Hellenic world, giving way reluctantly, but without much resistance, before the cataclysm of Christianity.' Yet those blasts, says Harrison, have 'the authentic snarl of a man trapped physically in poverty and persecution'. No poet has ever been so isolated nor so bitter.

If variants of the drama in *Refrains and Choruses* can be found in all Birtwistle's work, nowhere is it more explicit than in *Punch and Judy* (18). No protagonist can ever have been so wilful or capricious as Mr Punch. No one could have been so disruptive. In the opera, however, Birtwistle introduces a character not found in the traditional entertainment: Choregos, the showman himself. In Greek theatre, Choregos was the name given to the person who sponsored the chorus, but because of the word-association, Birtwistle makes him the chorus's leader. The

---

* Tony Harrison, *Palladas—Poems* (Anvil Press, 1975), Preface.

*peripeteia* occurs when Punch shuts Choregos in a bass viol case and gleefully saws him in half. Thereafter comes the nightmare when Punch's victims turn against him, at least in his mind. Unconsciously he realizes that without Choregos there is nothing for him to react against. He is impotent. In that moment, Birtwistle asserts that protagonist and chorus, the capricious and the staid, chance and necessity are symbiotic. They need each other.

All Birtwistle's music involves role-playing, all his turning points are role exchanges. As a clarinetist he was acutely conscious that performers are like actors. They do not give of themselves, they realize and project an assumed character. Composers like playwrights write material to be performed and the best of them know that musicians and actors need parts in which the character is larger than life. Discovery of medieval techniques and a central organizing principle were only two of the factors which opened the floodgates. Equally important was the discovery that music is not an abstract activity involving the manipulation of notes on paper; it is something concrete, real and eminently practical.

# 2: 1958–65

SO IMPRESSED WAS THE Society for the Promotion of New Music with *Refrains and Choruses* that it decided to include it in its concert at the 1959 Cheltenham Festival, one of the most prestigious events in its calendar. On hearing the news, Birtwistle took a characteristically bold and extreme step—he sold his clarinets. From now on all his musical activity would be devoted to composition: performing would no longer present an alternative course, even though this necessitated earning a living less congenially. During the year before Cheltenham he moved twenty miles outside London to Slough, working first in a pharmaceutical factory 'churning out pills on a production line', then as a salesman for an asbestos firm. In his spare time he analysed Stravinsky.

As composing from the top of his head was out of character, he required a system, a *modus operandi*, but this was not found overnight; it took him seven years of trial and error. For not until *Tragoedia* (14), composed in 1965, were the final pieces fitted into place. Since then there may have been a change in mood, but no fundamental change in technique has occurred.

Stravinsky, the composer who could 'invent a tool to fashion the wood', was the starting point, and the piece which particularly took Birtwistle's fancy was the ballet *Agon* (1957). He subjected it to the most detailed analysis he has ever undertaken and echoes of it still reverberate in his music. It is one of a group of pieces composed during the mid-fifties in which

17

Stravinsky introduces serial elements. 'Yet serial music never actually touched him', says Birtwistle; he used the elements not to be up to date, not to be new, but '*to invent an archaic world*'. This is so important to Birtwistle that it must be amplified.

*Agon* consists of a series of dances modelled after examples in a French dance manual of the mid-seventeenth century; but it is not pastiche. Stravinsky has not recreated a past style, he has invented one. So authentic seem his dances, so original, they could be the source rather than the aftermath of the genre. This being the case, a circular process is implied; at any stage a composer can initiate the historic process again, start from the beginning. In other words, inventing an archaic world serves the same purpose as constructing an isorhythmic cycle—it suggests perpetual recurrence. Birtwistle is fascinated by the idea.

*Punch and Judy*, for instance, is referred to as a source opera, a work considered a prototype for all other operas, a work 'which, though written after other operas, would give the illusion of having been written before them'. So it is with all his works: each could have preceded itself.

But Stravinsky's influence is not confined to this; it extends to such specific details as additive rhythms, the hard-edged contour of lines, the central premise that 'all music is nothing more than a succession of impulses' converging on 'a definite point of repose', not least, the constant need for polar attraction.

Nowhere is this more vividly illustrated than in scoring. *Agon* abounds in unusual ensembles: violin, xylophone and two trombones; cello, mandoline, harp and two trumpets. Yet the balancing of these bizarre groupings, the sensitivity of Stravinsky's ear in selecting the polar attraction of each cord, each phrase, each section, is masterly. If Birtwistle learned nothing else from *Agon*, he learned how to balance an ensemble, a texture, how to hear what Stravinsky calls 'the essential axes of music'.* In the two commemorative pieces he composed for him, *Chorale from a Toy-Shop* (19) and *Tombeau in Memoriam Igor Stravinsky* (40), the proof is displayed. Only the acutest of inner ears could have conceived them.

---

*Igor Stravinsky, *Poetics of Music* (Harvard University Press, 1947), p. 35.

Even so his tonal language is as simple as may be. Essentially he acknowledges only three intervals, the perfect intervals of octave, fifth and fourth. All others lean into these: the ninths and sevenths into the octave, the sixths and fourths into the fifth, the fifths and thirds into the fourth and the seconds into the unison. Basically they are embellishments, appoggiaturas. The opening of the piece he composed when he returned to London to be a music copyist after the success he received in Cheltenham, *Monody for Corpus Christi* (2), will illustrate the point. On the surface it looks fairly elaborate but in essence it is only the embellishment of the cadential fifth—the pole of attraction (the point of repose) being the B of the horn.

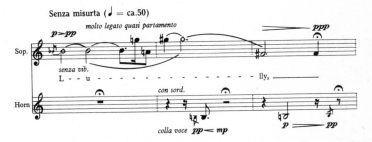

These notes come from superimposing and interlocking two versions of the basic melodic cell. By distributing them asymmetrically across three octaves, he opens up possibilites for development, but once the underlying structure has been grasped, its intervals, even the rising seventh and falling ninth, can be 'heard' with comparative ease.

Birtwistle's next point of repose comes at the end of the introductory section and consists of the notes F and C, as indicated within the brackets. Technically the whole passage could be considered an example of melismatic organum with the

19

horn functioning as *vox principalis* (principal voice) and the soprano as *vox organalis* (the added voice). Bearing in mind that all Birtwistle's music, no matter how dense and rich it may be, is essentially monody, it was inevitable that it would be thickened by the medieval practice of organum, the doubling of the line at the octave, fifth or fourth. In his early music, where he aims to be as fluid as possible, he uses almost exclusively florid or melismatic organum, but later, notably from *Ring a Dumb Carillon* (12) onwards, he is prepared to be really simple. The following is the beginning of a long passage which dominates the central section of *The Fields of Sorrow* (39) later to occur (amended) in *The Triumph of Time* (43). It is free organum; parallel motion at the fourth made livelier by crossing the parts.

Usually Birtwistle's use of organum is less obvious than this and involves imperfect rather than perfect octaves, fifths and fourths—adjacencies, in other words. Sometimes organum will be added to organum so that the texture becomes even richer. A simple illustration is his arrangement of Machaut's *Hoquetus David* (30) where the monody (the *cantus firmus*) is already enriched by two-part counterpoint; to each of the three voices he adds a bell-like quint, an exact reproduction at the fifth. Thus the single line has proliferated into six.

In *Monody for Corpus Christi* it proliferates into four, those for soprano, flute, violin and horn. The idea for the piece came from Holst's *Four Songs for Voice and Violin*, Op. 35. One summer's evening during the First World War, seemingly, Holst went into Thaxted Parish Church where a woman was wandering up and down the aisles singing to the accompaniment of the open strings of a violin she carried. The bare fifths framed her song and helped to articulate it. For Birtwistle this was analogous with his own methods. Like Holst, he sets medieval texts, but he arranges them to form the kind of cycle discussed earlier: that is, the import of the first movement (a vision of Christ as a dead knight) comes after that of the last (a lullabye to the infant Jesus). Between them is an apocalyptic fanfare for the instruments alone. Once again the horn plays the role of protagonist: once again it returns to the collective at the end.

Although extremely elaborate, *Monody for Corpus Christi* made an even deeper impression than *Refrains and Choruses*, for it was selected to represent Britain at the 1961 Festival of the International Society for Contemporary Music.

His next piece, *Three Sonatas for Nine Instruments* (3), fared less well. It was scheduled for an SPNM concert at the 1960 Aldeburgh Festival but after the first rehearsal he withdrew it. Scores and parts must be somewhere, but no one can say where. To Birtwistle's relief, they appear to be lost.

The piece was an exercise in symmetries, but they turned out to be too obvious, there were not sufficient irregularities in them. Symmetries were implicit in Birtwistle's music from the start and even though they were misconceived on this occasion they ultimately became an important ingredient of his style. Isorhythm, for instance, constitutes rotational symmetry—*talea* and *color* rotate around a notional axis, each, to use the technical jargon, being carried into itself; the basic melodic cell constitutes bilateral symmetry—the note above the starting point mirrored by the note below it; finally, the basic rhythmic cell, the heartbeat, forms translational symmetry when repeated—it is symmetrically translated from one area of time to another. Of the three, undoutedly the most useful has been bilateral symmetry. Not only can it be used around a horizontal axis (the predominant one in music), but also around a vertical one. To understand Birtwistle's use of it we must leap ahead to what he has to say in his sleeve note for the gramophone record of *Tragoedia* (14). Here he is discussing symmetry around a vertical axis, but his remarks could equally apply to the other more usual variety.

The essence of the work's structure is symmetry—more specifically, bilateral symmetry in which concentric layers are grouped outward from a static central pillar [Parados (A) Episodion[1] (B) Stasimon (C) Episodion[2] (B) Exodos (A)]... Although the Episodion[1] is symmetrically complete in the small, it is also part of a large symmetry which is not yet complete. This is what impels the music forward across the central Stasimon and into the second Episodion. Symmetry may be seen retrospectively as a static phenomenon; but incomplete symmetry, that is, symmetry in process of being formed, is dynamic because it creates a structural need that eventually must be satisfied.

Having stated why symmetry is so crucial, he then goes on to outline the irregularities he inserts in order to ensure closure and avoid boredom:

The second Episodion begins the return journey. It is a mirror-image of the first only to the extent that it reverses the characters: 'peaceful—peaceful— violent' becomes 'violent—violent—peaceful'. Apart from this reversal, the internal content of the first Episodion is freely rearranged...

He then goes on to mention even more extensive changes and concludes:

The non-literal symmetry that results from all these changes is crucial since an exact mirror structure, even though motivated earlier in the work, would limit the form unnecessarily to one dimension as the work drew to a close.

The prototype for *Tragoedia* was the piece Birtwistle wrote immediately after the failure of *Three Sonatas for Nine Instruments*, a piece which by its very title indicates his desire for punctilliousness and discipline: *Précis* for solo piano (4). With it he tried to write a piece 'which turned back on itself yet had a sense of forward movement'. In other words, like *Tragodeia*, it is symmetrical (A B C B A) but alters its return journey so as to generate energy towards climax and closure. Actually it is stricter, more literal in its mirror images and more scrupulous concerning its symmetry across the horizontal axis than the later piece. This is apparent even in the wildly inaccurate printed score.

It was composed just before Birtwistle moved to the borders of Dorset and Wiltshire to teach woodwind instruments in four different private schools: Cranborne Chase, a fashionable girls' boarding school in Wardour Castle, and three preparatory schools—Claysmore and Knighton House in Blandford and Port Regis near Shaftesbury. He had recently married and his wife Sheila and he had started a family (the first of three sons); a more stable income than that provided by music copying was therefore required.

During his first term there he arranged for his pupils some four-part canzonas by the Renaissance composer Heinrich Isaac. On this occasion he probably learned more from the exercise than his pupils, for in the canzonas the tune (usually a chanson melody) is placed not in the topmost voice but in the tenor. This was also the case with early German chorales, those by Johann Walter for instance. The appeal was that the tune, the most important element of the piece, became obscured by the texture surrounding it. At the same time, Birtwistle happened to go to the Picasso exhibition running at the Tate. There he came across the series of pictures in which Picasso expands or exploits certain obscure details discovered in Velasquez's *Las Meninas*: the outline of a dog perhaps, a trick of perspective. The coincidence produced two works: one, *The World is Discovered* for double wind quintet, guitar and harp, was produced rapidly, the other, *Chorales*, his first orchestral piece, slowly. For three years he laboured at it and then had to wait another four for a performance. But although still neglected, it constitutes a watershed in his progress.

*The World is Discovered* (5) is not a study for it—'I don't write studies for anything', he claims—but could be considered its satellite. Inconspicuous details from five of Isaac's canzonas are blown up in the Picassian manner. None is intended to be recognized, the exercise being for the composer rather than the listener. Attention can therefore be focused on the succession of verse and refrain cast almost exclusively in rhythmical unisons. The music is still monody enriched by organum, but now the lines move in contrary motion so that polyphony and homophony are one and the same. Yet which voice is *principalis*, which *organalis* is obscure; monody cannot be distinguished from proliferation.

Birtwistle was well into *Chorales* (7) when he came across the painting by Pieter Brueghel the Elder which became associated with the work: *The Martyrdom of St Catherine*. This too obscures its nominal subject. The eye encounters first and foremost a typical Renaissance landscape: close at hand rolling hills, beyond, higher slopes, in the distance the sea and a fishing village; everywhere the routine of daily life—farmers in their fields, sailors mending boats. Only after considerable scrutiny can St Catherine be found. Thereafter the viewer must stand back from the canvas and note that her death is only a detail among details, that the daily round takes precedence.

In *Chorales* Birtwistle adopts a more humanistic approach than Brueghel: he dramatizes the search and gives the discovery climatic emphasis. The piece is described as a landscape in which the ear may focus attention equally on a number of different musical levels, with the chorale idea as an opposed but increasingly integrated element. Roger Smalley says the work 'vibrates with energy and ideas and there is never a moment which is not full of aural fascination'.* Almost the whole of the large body of instruments is in constant use and provides 'a "landscape" of tremendous depth and subtlety. The cores of this shimmering mass of intricate detail are the chorales—the "acts", sometimes obliterated by the density and interest of their surroundings, sometimes becoming the focus of attention themselves'. (In this context, the word 'act' refers to the essential action—the act of St Catherine's martyrdom, for instance). Smalley continues:

* Roger Smalley, 'Birtwistle's Chorales', *Tempo*, Spring 1967, pp. 25-7.

A chorale is a single melodic line doubled at various intervals (harmonized) in rhythmic unison—in other words it is a whole series of vertical 'acts' (chords). It is this conception of a chorale which Birtwistle has utilized in this piece, most obviously in the fourth section where a single melodic line is doubled at many intervals played in rhythmic unison. Other events take place between these massive chords (passing notes) while in earlier sections melodic lines tend to proliferate from the chorales (chorale prelude).

Smalley observes that all the horizontal and vertical pitch formations, the general shape of each section, and the whole work follow a wedge-shaped pattern. Wedge-shaped patterns are again not new. They occur in *Refrains and Choruses* for instance—indeed, the build-up to the climax of that piece is based upon a gradual expansion of the basic melodic cell (E F D sharp) spiralling upwards and downwards (E F D sharp F sharp D natural G C sharp . . .) to form the prototype wedge. On completion the process can either repeat itself or turn backwards to its starting point. It is symmetry *par excellence* and in *Chorales* the process is established as a principle, never abandoned, though never quite so blatantly obvious. In later works, even when the wedge becomes the *color* of the piece, the fact is disguised by redistribution. (For an example, turn to the opening of Chapter six, where *La Plage* is discussed.)

The drama of *Chorales*, like the drama of all Birtwistle's music, follows classical precedents in that it moves towards a moment combining recognition and reversal. The search for the chorale creates the tension, the recognition of it the climax, at which stage the structure turns back to its point of maximum repose, its starting point, here the sound of high pitchless percussion. During the last of the four sections, each of which has gone through the same material from a different perspective, Birtwistle at last introduces the chorale in block chords, intermittently and softly at first, more continuously and louder later. When the climax is reached, all accretions, all proliferations are stripped away, the harmony thins to multiple octave doublings, then unisons. F sharp, the initial pitch and constant pole of attraction, blazons forth triumphantly.

By now it must be evident that the visual arts contribute a great deal to Birtwistle's music. Mention has already been made of Cézanne, of Picasso and Brueghel; later Dürer and Paul Klee's names will appear, Klee's frequently. It may be no exaggeration to say that of all composers Birtwistle is probably the most deeply affected by visual things, not only paintings but visual objects of all kinds: landscapes, fossils, maps and films being but a few. He calls his pieces 'musical landscapes', his sections 'objects'. He talks of frozen frames, of labyrinths. At every level, visual arrangements provide ideas, suggest ways to proceed. Indeed, his genius is his ability to adapt the visual to the aural. For years his musical bible was not the String Quartets of Beethoven or some musical textbook, but Paul Klee's *Pedagogical Sketchbook*. Even Klee's opening sentences, referring to a beautifully curling line, were an inspiration: 'An *active* line on a walk, moving freely, without goal. A walk for a walk's sake.'* It was Klee who reminded him, after the debacle of *Three Sonatas for Nine Instruments*, that non-symmetrical balance, the equalization of unequal but equivalent parts, is more useful than exact bilateral conformity.

It was also Klee (though not in *The Pedagogical Sketchbook*) who gave him ideas about the presentation of objects in different contexts and the uses of juxtaposition. Before completing *Chorales*, he had wanted to write a large-scale vocal piece about the seasons and a 'song-book for instruments' was being assembled for possible inclusion. It never materialized, but items from the song-book appeared as *Entr'actes* (6), a piece intended as a companion to Debussy's Sonata for flute, viola and harp. Here the five movements are 'five different visions of the same object', but what would happen, Birtwistle asked himself, if these visions were placed within a different context? If Klee were to be followed then a new background would offer other perspectives. He therefore expanded the original piece into

* Paul Klee, *The Pedagogical Sketchbook* (Faber and Faber, 1968), p. 16.

26

*Entr'actes and Sappho Fragments* (11). By adding five songs to texts by the Greek poetess and interspersing between them new versions of the entr'actes, 'a chemical change takes place', he says, 'something strange happens to the entr'actes in the new context'.

To enhance the transformation, he specifies a particular platform arrangement; for the first time, he uses the visual to intensify the aural. In this expanded version of the piece, violin, oboe and percussion as well as a singer are added to the ensemble. The performers are asked to sit in a semi-circle, the flautist at one extreme, the singer at the other. These two, the carriers of the foreground interest (*vox principalis* or *vox organalis*, whatever the case may be) are requested to stand; foreground and changing background are thus clearly differentiated.

Even without the benefit of hindsight, one can see the direction in which all these interests and activities are going. The intensification of dramatic forms and now the involvement of the visual strongly suggest opera. And so it was. In August 1964, shortly after the first performance of *Entr'actes and Sappho Fragments* at the Cheltenham Festival, Goehr, Maxwell Davies and Birtwistle inaugurated the first of two summer schools of music which they held under the presidency of Michael Tippett at Wardour Castle. As it happened, the talk, certainly in private, was of opera. Unlike the situation on the continent where opera had become *de trop*, Britain was experiencing an operatic renaissance. Two years earlier Tippett had won approval with *King Priam* and was now well and truly embarked on *The Knot Garden*; Maxwell Davies had virtually completed the first act of *Taverner*, while Goehr was mulling over *Arden Must Die*. Both Richard Rodney Bennett and Malcolm Williamson had produced operas that year, and Britten, the doyen of them all in this field, had unveiled *Curlew River*, the first of his church parables. Clearly British composers, even young ones, had no reservations about the anecdotal or the referential!

Characteristically, Birtwistle chose a subject that is not high art but working-class: Punch and Judy—the oldest urban entertainment still performed. Capable of a variety of interpretations, yet devoid of a linear plot, it suited his purposes admirably. For months he pored over documents about it in the British Museum, then when his ideas were almost set he invited the American pianist Stephen Pruslin to be his librettist. According to Pruslin, what they were *not* trying to do was write a children's opera faithful to the puppet play.

> Anyone who has witnessed that entertainment in its usual fairground or seaside setting will know there is very little an operatic version could add to the cogent and forceful original. No, what we wanted was something quite different: a stylized and ritualistic drama for adults that used all of the imagery, the trappings and paraphernalia of the original as a departure-point. In fact we wanted to have our cake and eat it: to write a work that would enable an audience of adults to re-experience the vividness of their childhood reactions during the performance while allowing enough scope for interpretive speculation afterwards.*

Birtwistle delayed tackling the music until the libretto was completed and a crucial problem related to dramatic pacing had been solved. Up to then, in order to be as fluid as possible, his music had involved additive rhythms—the rhythmic organization cultivated by Stravinsky (particularly in *The Rite of Spring*) and Messiaen. That is, instead of dividing and multiplying durations to produce a regular pattern, they are added or subtracted to produce something irregular. Thus measurement has been forfeited and fluidity prevails. In practice, the method usually involves the manipulation of rhythmical cells, their contraction and expansion, the alteration of their proportions.

Among avant-garde composers of the fifties and early-sixties, however, there grew the urge to make music more fluid than even additive rhythms provided. Boulez talked of musical time as being 'pulsed' either regularly or irregularly:

---

* Sleeve-note for the Decca recording.

But there is also a kind of music that can do entirely without pulsations—a music that seems to float, and in which the writing itself makes it impossible for the performer to keep in line with a pulsed tempo: grace notes, ornaments, or a profusion of differences in dynamics will make the performer give so much attention to what is happening that temporal control recedes into the background.*

This is precisely what Birtwistle achieved in *Précis* which he had modelled on *Quantitäten*, a piece by the avant-garde Swedish composer Bo Nilsson. By alternating between extremely fast gestures and motionless notes, by constantly changing tempo, this too seemed to float.

Faced with the prospect of writing an opera in which temporal events must be timed to a nicety, such techniques needed to be amended. In opera, control is paramount. If his drama were to be paced, pulse would have to be reinstated. But he was not prepared to abandon his fluid additive practice. Once again he wanted to have his cake and eat it. He therefore decided to apply his central organizing principle to the situation, the operation whereby the predictable is pitted against the unpredictable, whereby pulse, something absolutely regular, undifferentiated and therefore mechanical, is set against irregular, highly differentiated and organic additive rhythm. It has proved to be one of his most fertile syntheses.

The first fruits, *Ring a Dumb Carillon* (12) and *Tragoedia* (14), are two of his finest pieces. Hitherto his music had elicited a favourable but passive reaction from the critics. Robert Henderson's was typical 'A music of delicately poised nuance, of an essential lyricism...'† With these two works comes a positive response. David Drew calls *Tragoedia* 'an earthy drama: protestant, rude, and generally at odds with traditional orders of thought and behaviour'.‡ Even though there remains a still

---

* Pierre Boulez, *Conversations with Célestin Deliège* (Eulenburg, 1976), p. 69.
† Robert Henderson, 'Harrison Birtwistle', *Musical Times*, March 1964, p. 189.
‡ Sleevenote for EMI recording.

centre of lyricism, 'blood is shed'. Henceforth, Birtwistle's reputation becomes associated with violence rather than nuance.

Not that there is violence in *Ring a Dumb Carillon*: what it manifests is the control Birtwistle has gained over rapid changes of pace, his ability to change gear effectively. A passage from near the beginning of the piece (p. 4 of the score) will illustrate the point. Scored for soprano, clarinet and percussion, the monody lies with the clarinet, a situation obscured by having the soprano sing the interesting text in rhythmical unison with it.

Fifths are diminished or stretched to sixths, fourths augmented or narrowed to thirds, but the passage is in free organum; the independence of the parts stemming from contrary notion.

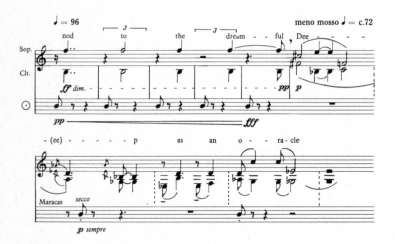

To get from the faster to the slower tempo as smoothly as possible, Birtwistle changes gear twice. First, against the insistent pulse of the suspended cymbal, he writes out a ritardando in the soprano and clarinet; then he eases into the new tempo with a bar of triplets, each unit being roughly the same as the pulse of the previous section. Once into his tempo, the maracas establish a six-beat pulse while the soprano and clarinet revolve in additive rhythms. Using the basic cell of the heartbeat six variants are given. Thus dry, mechanical pulse is laid against something organic.

Another aspect of Birtwistle's new practice, however, is only hinted at, that is his use of rhythmic adjacencies. Just as notes surrounding the basic intervals are counted as surrogates, so too are those surrounding a pulse. In both instances the substitutes are selected either by chance or to conform to some numerical pattern. In effect, the free parts bend the pulse as in jazz. The relationship enhances their unpredictability, their seeming freedom.

With *Tragoedia* these innovations are developed still further, the most striking being the variety of pace Birtwistle achieves. The range from hectic bustle to absolute stillness is made possible only by control of pace. Earlier his comments about the work's symmetry were quoted. From these, it must have been evident that the 'earthy, rude drama' is Greek in orientation. Each of the sub-titles refers to a section of Greek tragedy. His aim was to bridge the gap between 'absolute music' and theatre music:

> It contains a specific drama [he says] but this drama is purely musical. The title does not imply 'tragic' in the nineteenth century sense. 'Tragoedia' literally means 'goat-dance', and the work is concerned with the ritual and formal aspects of Greek tragedy rather than with the content of any specific play.

For the drama, he takes the conflict between the odd-man-out and the chorus, an idea left in abeyance since *Monody for Corpus Christi*. Here there are two outsiders, the horn from the work's wind quintet and the cello from its string quartet, the link between them provided by a harp. With these additional forces, Birtwistle can relate protagonist to chorus, chorus to chorus and protagonist to protagonist. Indeed, the Episodions, traditionally the sections between complete choral songs, are given over not only to the conflict between the two protagonists but also to the soaring love duet that emerges from it—an occasion Birtwistle was to recall when he quoted the passage six years later in *Meridian* (36).

*Tragoedia* is a turbulent piece, well named 'goat-dance', yet at its centre lies one of the stillest, most tranquil movements in all Birtwistle, a moment of Apollonian serenity in the midst of Dionysian raucousness. Paradoxically, his newly-found control has provided him with the means to retard the velocity of his music as well as increase it. For this movement he uses the word 'Stasimon' not merely to indicate the separation between two distinct sections of his drama, but because it formally implies stasis, 'the still centre of the turning world'.

Those who heard *Tragoedia* when it was first performed at the 1965 Wardour Castle Summer School have said they will never forget the excitement it generated. With it his career was assured.

## 3: VERSES FOR CLARINET AND PIANO

AT THIS STAGE IT may be useful to review Birtwistle's methods by considering in detail two of the eight *Verses* for clarinet and piano (15) which he wrote in autumn 1965 for a concert given by Alan Hacker and Stephen Pruslin. The sketches have been lost and Birtwistle can no longer remember how he arrived at some of the details, but the work was composed before his use of random numbers, so that most of the procedures can be traced back to source. He wrote it with great care and it provides an ideal summary of his technique at that time. The felicitous canon of the sixth verse is still a source of pride.

Alan Hacker says:

> Harry was particularly sensitive about writing for the clarinet, being a clarinettist, and he wanted to let time pass in order to forget his own clarinet playing with its limitations before he actually wrote clarinet music . . . We only had the last movement delivered to us on the afternoon of the concert; Harry said that he wrote it on the train up from Wiltshire, although it looked a bit too neat for that! . . . *Verses* is actually a very strong piece despite its restraints.

Restraint is its outstanding feature, and it is characteristically extreme. After the noisy turbulence of *Tragoedia*'s goat-dance, Birtwistle has composed a piece in which the pianist holds the soft pedal down throughout and the general dynamic level rarely rises above *pianissimo*. For the clarinettist it is an exercise in control rather than dexterity. At times the player has to play so quietly that his sound can hardly be distinguished from the background. These two factors, control and inconspicuousness, are the main issues.

Birtwistle conceives all his music theatrically. It is not merely dramatic in the sense that Beethoven's music is dramatic; it is as if the platform were a stage and the players *dramatis personae*. His first task, therefore, is to set the scene and locate the players within it; his second is to establish their characters. Since drama requires conflict, in both these areas there must be strong contrasts. Control is therefore contrasted with waywardness, inconspicuousness with prominence. However, although drama results from character clashes, character itself is immutable, so that resolution must lie in the other area. Inconspicuousness and prominence can be interpreted as referring to status, in this particular context the status of accompanist and soloist. If the clarinettist starts as accompanist and the pianist as soloist the position can be changed. Status is mutable. In practice, the assumption at a clarinet recital is that the clarinettist is the soloist and the pianist the accompanist, so the change would fulfil expectations. The platform, then, is a stage on which two characters, although stationary, can, by virtue of the material given them and the nature of their instruments, move from foreground to background positions at will.

The difference between a clarinet and a piano can be assessed in various ways, but Birtwistle selects control as the deciding factor on the grounds that a clarinettist is able to vary the dynamic level and quality of a note after it has started whereas a pianist cannot. The characteristics he assigns to the instruments are steadfastness and waywardness insofar as they display control or the lack of it. Verse one consists of the clarinettist steadfastly playing one note five times in exactly the same way, while the pianist waywardly spreads many notes across five octaves in almost careless abandon. By virtue of the difference in interest and definition, the clarinettist will be deemed to be in the background, the pianist in the foreground. (Verse one can be found on p. 38.)

Having established the contrasts, Birtwistle must next introduce conflict. This he does by having the second verse played by the clarinet alone. Its material is mainly that previously given to the piano; it takes on some of the piano's waywardness, and it usurps its position in the foreground. Yet response has been given and a dialogue can take place. Thereafter the drama consists of how one character will afffect the other, how their relative statuses will alter and how these will eventually lead to the canon of the sixth verse, where the two are on more or less equal terms. That will be a moment of recognition; afterwards, the two can act in harmony rather than conflict, and the statuses normally ascribed to them at a recital can be accepted without rivalry.

The key to the resolution of the situation is this act of recognition. Recognition is the crux of Greek tragedy, and given Birtwistle's passion for Greek theatre it is not surprising that he should want to fashion his drama in the classical manner. In *Tragoedia* he had used the formal divisions of Greek tragedy; here he engages the two most decisive elements of tragic plot: *peripeteia* (reversal or turning point) and *anagnorisis* (recognition or discovery). Recognition is always recognition of a person's identity and it emerges out of a sudden switch from one state of affairs to its opposite. Birtwistle's reversal comes in verse five. Until then the material had been growing more and more profusely. Suddenly the proliferations are cast away and only the bare bones remain.

The act of reversing or turning is fundamental to Birtwistle as we discovered when discussing *Refrains and Choruses* and *Punch and Judy*. In *The Mask of Orpheus* (60), which is his longest and most elaborate piece to date, turning is not merely a technical device, it is the issue of the drama. One of the reasons for choosing 'verses' as a title for the present work is that turning is the meaning of the word's etymological root. He was delighted that originally *versus* meant a furrow, a turning of the plough, and that it only later referred to a line of writing, a turning of the head or eye. He finds in both these acts an analogy with what happens in his music. Although he unfolds a plot or narrative, he advances it by turning back to the start again. Each verse goes over the same territory as preceding ones, only from a different angle.

Even their internal organization follows this course. In the first verse, where the basic material is given to the piano, the overall structure is an isorhythmic cycle, one complete turn of the isorhythmic wheel. Both *talea* and *color*, however, are irregular. Instead of repeating the same pattern of durations and pitches exactly, as would have happened in medieval music, Birtwistle modifies them as if he were considering each from a new perspective. His *talea* is the throb of the heartbeat (ú—); his *color* a simple oscillation around a central note, in this case E, the note which lies at the centre of the keyboard (E F E flat). In medieval music a cycle would have consisted of three appearances of the *talea* and two of the *color* before the pattern started again; here, the modifications necessitate that, although the *color* appears twice, the *talea* shall appear four times. This would be the medieval prototype:

Now follow Birtwistle's modifications. To make the iambic rhythm more pervasive, he augments the second and fourth cells to twice their length, so that high groupings are achieved:

To make an even higher grouping, however, he reverses the rhythm. By contracting the fourth cell and expanding the second further, he creates a grouping which is diametrically opposite to the iambic. Instead of short-long (∪—), it becomes the trochaic long-short (—∪).

(The issue of reversing ryhthmic grouping is thoroughly discussed in *The Rhythmic Structure of Music* by Grosvenor Cooper and Leonard Meyer which was published by the University of Chicago Press in 1960 and widely read by composers at that time. The authors would have argued that for closure the high-level trochaic grouping needs to be changed into an iamb. This is how Birtwistle organizes the last verse.)

The most idiosyncratic aspect of the heartbeat rhythm, however, is not the relative length of the two units, but the fact that the first is stressed. Birtwistle reinforces the beginning of the trochee not by dynamic weight but by applying to the first two cells ornaments in the form of arpeggiation between the hands and grace-notes, so that with these additional heartbeats the first half of the cycle has much greater weight and therefore greater stress.

The *color* is also modified, but as there is only one repetition within the cycle, the changes are confined to two. In the first unit he adds an E between the second and third notes so that the undulation becomes smoother. In the second the notes are inverted.

E F (E) E flat  :  E D sharp F

As it is Birtwistle's tenet that a musical object should be looked at from different perspectives not only sequentially but also simultaneously, he doubles this monody first at the fourth above, then at the fourth below, and finally, reaching over to an

37

additional note on the clarinet, to the fourth above again. He thus creates free organum. The exception to the pattern of a fourth either side is the penultimate A, a deviation which in context gives the impression that the process may shortly unfold and burgeon.

|  |  |  |  |  |  | B flat (clarinet) |
|--------|---|-----|----------|----------|---|---|
| B flat | A |     |          |          |   |   |
| E F    |   | (E) | E flat: E | D sharp  | F |   |
|        |   |     | B flat B | A sharp  | (A) |   |

When scattered across five octaves the monody passes from right hand to left then back again. In the prcoess, imitative counterpoints appear such as the falling E to B flat in the right hand which is echoed almost immediately in the left hand. The function of the clarinet during this capricious activity is to provide a regular pulse for the rhythms and an axis of symmetry for the pitch. That, at least, would seem to be the intended function, but it is not fulfilled, for the pulse seems to drift away from the piano's additive rhythms as if it were on a different plane, and its pitch causes the symmetry to shift markedly off keel. Thus the structure is neither coordinated nor balanced and consequently posseses dynamism.

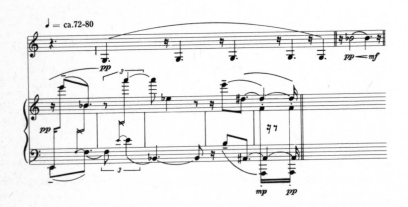

It may be recalled that Birtwistle in his notes for *Tragoedia* said: 'incomplete symmetry, that is symmetry in process of being formed, is dynamic because it creates a structural need that eventually must be satisfied'. Verse one has only seven pitch classes. Expressed as a scale, the clarinet's G is at the centre and is manifestly the axis of bilateral symmetry: E flat E F — G — A B flat B. When Birtwistle distributes these notes across five octaves, however, he so arranges it that the axis of symmetry is not G but E above middle C, or rather, a point just below this E. The repeated Gs do not stabilize the structure but throw it off balance. It is only when the detached B flat sounds at the very end that a more or less even keel is attained. The mid-way point between the G and B flat is a point between the D and E flat above middle C, so that the balance is not quite equal; but this lack of equality keeps the structure open. It would be inept to resolve the ambiguity too soon.

The detached B flat actually has a number of functions. Birtwistle imbues everything with structural depth; he considers all aspects of his score from as many angles as possible. As well as having a harmonic function, the B flat punctuates the verse, links up with the last high E on the piano so that the opening E to B flat is echoed once again, and not least, it initiates what can only be called a musical rhyming scheme.

The word 'verse' also has structural depth. In farming it may have meant a furrow, but in poetry it can be used for either the rhythmical unit or a line of the rhyming unit of a stanza. Birtwistle manages to involve both meanings. All his verses are complete in themselves (each is a three-phrase musical sentence). In that sense they are stanzas. But they are also like separate lines of a single large-scale stanza: an eight-line stanza of two quatrains. These are defined by the melodic pattern formed by adding together each concluding note of the clarinet. A rhyming scheme, however, is not a pattern of pitches but of timbres. However, Birtwistle has only two timbres at his disposal so he must call on dynamics to serve instead. Four other verses, as well as the first, end with detached notes. All entail the clarinet making a crescendo from *pianissimo* to *mezzo-forte*. This crescendo is the rhyme. But Birtwistle slightly alters the pattern at the end in order to draw the last two verses together. He initiates the crescendo in verse seven and completes it in verse eight.

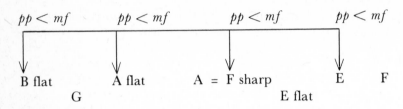

There is still at least one more function given to the final B flat of the first verse, and that has to do with its theatrical effect. In context it sounds not unlike a fanfare. When Birtwistle came to write *Verses for Ensembles* (25) some three years later in 1968, he had two trumpets moved to the back of the stage to deliver fanfares in a not dissimilar manner. In the present piece the crescendo seems to herald an entrance of importance. It is the entrance of the protagonist: none other than the clarinettist himself. Aurally he strides to stage centre to deliver a monody. In the Greek theatre a monody was a solo song placed in association with the opening parados for chorus. Birtwistle has clearly designated that if the clarinettist has the role of soloist, the pianist, who plays a harmony instrument capable of covering a number of 'voices', must take the role of chorus. This would comply with the musical meaning of the word 'verses'—passages for a soloist in alternation with those for a choir, hence verse-anthem or versicle (alternation of officiant and congregation) and verset (the name given to a short organ solo alternating with a choir).

But the word 'chorus' has different meanings as well, and it is characteristic of Birtwistle that he would also want to involve them. It can mean either a body of performers or a refrain. As the work unfolds it becomes apparent that whereas the solo verses are each given a new identity, the chorus verses change relatively little. They become refrains answering the call of the soloist. Yet the pattern of call and response is achieved only at the end. Until then the order has been the other way round: response has preceded call. Thus once again a reversal has taken place, a reversal which like the other has placed things in an expected order.

Verse two, being a solo verse, is longer and more substantial than the first; yet no new material is added. To produce length, Birtwistle goes back over the previous verse, first forwards then backwards. On his forward journey he picks out certain notes from the upper line traced by the piano and clarinet; on the return he selects notes from the lower line, but instead of going backwards in a straight line from right to left, he returns in loops, extracting groups of four notes first from the end, then the middle, then the beginning, all of which are scanned from the usual left to right. Thus he deliberately involves himself in turning back—not once but thrice.

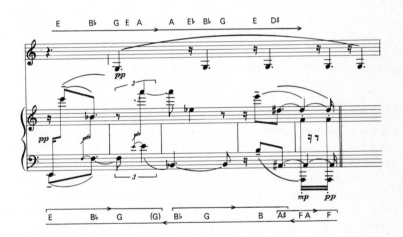

What Birtwistle extracts are intervals rather than specific pitches. When he comes to compose his second verse some of these pitches must be transposed if all twelve notes of the chromatic scale are to be involved. (Once transposed, pitches lose their identity, but intervals do not.) In verse one there are only seven pitch classes, but Birtwistle's tonal system normally uses the whole gamut. This is best labelled chromatic modality because the twelve chromatic notes are in constant use yet a strong pole of attraction, which is usually the central axis of symmetry, firmly holds them in place. Consequently, at no time does the harmony become atonal. In transposing, he must ensure that his pole of attraction is not too weak. This is why the notes surrounding G, the pole he now selects to be the real one, not the false one as before, are those most frequently repeated. These are given in square brackets; the letters in round brackets refer to the pitches selected from verse one and indicate the extent of the transposition. The asterisk indicates a deliberate error!

```
E           B          [A] [F sharp]   B          [G sharp]   C           [A]         [F sharp]   E flat      D
(E)         (B flat) :  (G) (E)         (A)   :    (A)         (E flat*)   (B flat)    (G)   :      (E)         (D sharp)

[G]         D          C [A flat]       D flat     B flat      [A]         [F]         B           [A flat]    [G]
(A sharp)   (F)   :    (A) (F)   :       (B flat)   (G)   :                 (E)         (B flat)    (G)
                                                     (B)        (A sharp):
```

If we now turn to verse two as it appears in the score, two features may surprise us about the realization of these pitches. The first is that the axis of symmetry, which should be the G above middle C, is never stated, only implied; the other that the five repeated Gs in the clarinet part of verse one are now five B flats, four of them grace-notes. What should not surprise us is the adroitness of the octave transposition so that the clarinet swings between its two most mellifluous registers, clarino and chalumeau.

In verse one the piano's waywardness was in no way controlled by the pulse of the clarinet, but here pulse is very much in evidence. The clarinet may be assigned the role of expressive soloist, but the character given it is still one of

steadfastness. Pulse is the factor which defines the trait, even though its presence is only implied. Throughout the verse there runs a constant pulse of a minim (half note) which is extended by a quaver (eighth note) at certain cadential junctions, just as at the end of lines in hymns and chorales there are occasional pauses.

Although the pulse is constant other than at these junctures, the clarinet rarely states it. Like a jazz musician playing a lazy blues, it articulates just before or, more usually, just after the beat. Unlike the jazz musician, however, Birtwistle controls the degree of earliness or lateness. These are to pulse what adjacencies are to pitch and can be structured in like manner. Let the first phrase suffice to illustrate the point.

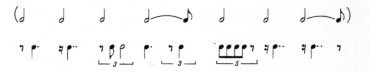

What has not been structured are dynamic marks and phrasing. These, says Birtwistle, are entirely the province of intuition. When he teaches composition, as he has done in the United States, one of the exercises he sets his students involves picking from a hat bits of paper which have a pitch and a duration written on them. He insists that the order in which they

43

appear should be preserved; the task is to make music from them. This can only be done by the use of dynamics and phrasing, but that, he maintains, is all the leeway the composer needs to create something of interest.

In this present piece, however, he gives himself more room to manoeuvre than the confines of dynamics and phrasing. In verse three, a choral verse in which the piano is predominant again, he freely amends some of the piano's waywardness by taking on board some of the clarinet's more disciplined material from verse two. Its line is folded into simultaneities; certain intervals are extended, others are contracted; there is greater conformity between the sections than in the first verse.

Verse four is another solo verse and in it there is another facet of Birtwistle's technique to examine, notably the way he expands a line both horizontally and vertically by the use of organum and the notes adjacent to the fourth, fifth and octave. Essentially he is expanding verse two, which was an unaccompanied monody. He now looks back at it to see if a harmonic context could be supplied and discovers a very Stravinskian solution. It we take just the first phrase, underpinning it lie two quite independent movements in fifths which come together at the end to form a cadence. Notes in the monody which do not fit the pattern of fifths are adjacencies which can be considered substitutes or appoggiature. The option is left open.

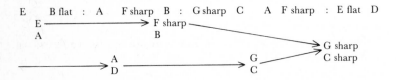

With this harmonic pattern at his disposal, Birtwistle can fill out his line with additional notes and chords, and make of them a frame in which the rhythm, articulated by the piano, is no longer a regular pulse with occasional elongations, but basically an alternation of 3/4 and 3/8 with a more protracted disturbance: three bars of 2/4.

Why one adjacency should be selected in preference to another or why these chords vary in number of notes they contain must remain a matter for speculation because Birtwistle cannot remember what determined them nor can they be traced back to source. When we come to discuss a similar passage in ... agm ... (54) for which sketches are extant, we shall discover that such decisions are the result of combining logical patterns with random numbers so that the consequence is bound to have a fortuitous element in it. This is the point: Birtwistle's purpose is to enrich the line and the texture with elements that are not open to ready explanation, but have an air of mystery about them.

Another reason might be that the purpose, in this particular instance, is to proliferate the material to such a degree that, like the monody in *Chorales*, the essential matter becomes hidden. When listening to the piece one certainly has the impression that the material has burgeoned almost willy-nilly. In the first verse, for example, the *color* had contained three notes, in the second the number has risen to eleven, now there are seventeen.

The next verse reverses this tendency, as already mentioned. Proliferations are pruned away and all that remains is the unadorned skeleton. It is a choral verse, but now the two parts have been swapped. The clarinet plays the piano's music but reduces it to only six notes, while the piano, gently and regularly, tolls the pulse—like a faraway bell. The tempo is very slow, the indication *senza expressione*.

Out of this reversal comes the moment of recognition embedded in the act of imitation, the clarinet leading, the piano following. The two instruments are now equal in both character and status. Yet they retain their instrumental identities. Two canons are involved. The most obvious is a rhythmic canon in which the piano disperses the clarinet's rhythms across three separate strands so as to produce a texture more appropriate to the keyboard than a single line would be. The other is a melodic canon quite independent of the first and more subterranean. For the most part it proceeds by inversion, but occasionally the notes are permutated as well.

Since the order of the last two verses is inverted the seventh is another solo verse and it continues the texture of the canon, but now the counterpoint has become freely imitative rather than strict, and it is the piano which leads, while the clarinet follows. Rhythmically, however, they are in unison as in verse four. The effect of having two similar verses in juxtaposition is to create a span of music which has a fairly uniform nature, a situation all finales strive to attain, as the rondos and fugues which end classical pieces bear witness.

After such homogeneity, the last verse sounds as if it were no more than a brief envoi, but it is actually the dénouement. The sequence of call and response (verse and refrain) is in its traditional order; and the relationship between clarinet and piano meets the demands of the recital situation without either of them sacrificing the characteristics assigned them. The clarinet, as soloist, exaggerates its capacity to control the dynamic gradations of a note, while the piano genuinely accompanies. In verse five it has articulated the five pulses strictly; now it renders them waywardly. Even so, they fit perfectly with what the clarinet is doing so there is no longer dramatic conflict between them; they are in harmony with each other.

There remains only one issue to resolve and this concerns pitch. Until the very last rhyming note, there are just six pitches. Yet even if they differ from the six in verse one, they still seem to be orientated around G. In the first verse G proved to be a deceptive axis of symmetry and B flat was needed to restore the balance. Here Birtwistle resorts to more traditional methods of establishing a tonal centre. The criterion is neither bilateral conformity nor 'the equalization of unequal but equivalent

parts'; it is part-writing. While the piano reiterates G A flat B, the clarinet pushes up from D to E. Great tension ensues, tension which can only be resolved by each part moving in contrary motion towards the other. Since we have now entered the province of tonality, it no longer matters in what octave the resolution appears. Loudly and brightly, two octaves higher than expected, the clarinet sounds it forth. It is the note which completes the rhyming scheme, and with it the drama is over.

# 4:  1966-70

EARLY IN 1966, shortly after writing *Verses* for clarinet and piano, Birtwistle won a Harkness Fellowship to study in the United States. After six years as a schoolmaster, he was to be a student once more. His first year was spent as a visiting fellow of Princeton University, where *Punch and Judy* was completed; the second took him to the University of Colorado at Boulder where he studied the analytical methods of Heinrich Schenker, an experience, he says, which proved invaluable when writing pastiche for productions at the National Theatre!

Not all of those two years was spent in the States, because it was in 1967 that he founded the Pierrot Players, which necessitated occasional visits to Britain. The later sixties was a period when the economic boom gave tremendous impetus to contemporary music. The BBC initiated Radio 3, its serious music network, and virtually tripled its contemporary music output; the Music Theatre Ensemble and the London Sinfonietta both almost entirely devoted to new music, were founded; and there was even a private electronic studio in Putney, no rival to institutions in Cologne or Milan, perhaps, but nevertheless a great encouragement to those interested in creating novel sounds and novel ways of producing them.

Birtwistle was involved with all of them. For the BBC he composed *Nomos* (22) and *Medusa* (31), for the Music Theatre Ensemble *Down by the Greenwood Side* (27) and for the London Sinfonietta *Verses for Ensembles* (25), the first of many works

49

written for that organization. *Medusa* also involved Peter Zinovieff's electronic studio.

Most of his efforts, however, were devoted to the Pierrot Players who, in a sense, blazed the trail. Although *Punch and Judy* had been accepted by the English Opera Group for production at the 1968 Aldeburgh Festival, Birtwistle felt that the established companies were too cumbersome for experimental activity in music theatre. What was required, he believed, was an organization small and flexible enough to mount limited music theatre in concert halls, rather than theatres, using the minimum of costumes, scenery, props and lighting.

The opportunity to found such an organization came with a commission from the Austrian Institute. He decided to write a theatre piece for the same combination of instruments used by Schonberg in *Pierrot Lunaire*, with the addition of a percussionist. Assisted by Alan Hacker, he auditioned the players and arranged a concert of limited theatre for the newly-opened Queen Elizabeth Hall. As well as *Pierrot Lunaire*, it included *Antechrist*, a curtain-raiser by Maxwell Davies (who was invited to become joint artistic director) and *Monodrama* (20), the commissioned piece.

*Monodrama*, unfortunately, did not fulfil expectations, and as time went on Birtwistle's enthusiasm for the Pierrot Players waned. He found it difficult to compose for a heterogeneous group of instruments, and became increasingly at odds with the high camp and sensationalism that was developing. Tension eventually came to a head in 1970, and he resigned. Nevertheless, in two pieces compsed during this period, *Medusa* (which was also written for the Pierrot Players) and *Verses for Ensembles*, he too succumbed to the fashion of the day: parody.

The name 'Medusa' has a two-fold significance. In Greek mythology it is the name of the girl, famed for her beautiful hair, who innocently desecrated a temple of Athene and was changed into a monster so ugly that whoever looked at her was turned to stone. She became a Gorgon, Athene replacing her hair with serpents. 'Medusa' is also the name of a jellyfish with similar tentacles. Birtwistle was particularly interested in D'Arcy Thompson's description of it: 'The living medusa has a geometrical symmetry so marked and regular as to suggest a physical or mechanical element in the little creature's growth and construction.'* It reproduces by detaching miniature replicas of itself from its tentacles. By combining these two meanings Birtwistle felt he could introduce the idea of parody in the form of distortion or mutilation without sacrificing his normal practice. The reproduction of the jellyfish could be taken as an analogy for the way he mechanically reproduces his *colores* and *taleae*, while the mutilation of the girl could symbolize the capricious, perhaps even the grotesque, way he 'bends' them.

He effects the mutilation not only with parody but also with electronics. There are strange synthesized sounds on one tape, while on another an alto saxophone bleats distortions of what is happening live. All the instruments are amplified—sometimes to a point of frenzy, as in the cadenzas for viola and cello. In this respect *Medusa* succeeds. It fares less well in its use of parody. It is the only piece in which Birtwistle borrows from other people and he found it difficult to integrate alien material with his own. He made two versions of the work, but neither satisfied him. On both occasions he borrowed from Bach. On the first he had an A-flat clarinet scream out a disfigured account of the chorale *Der Tag, der ist so freudenreich*, while for the much longer second version he alternated the chorale *Wer nur den lieben Gott lässt walten* with a parody of the chorale prelude *Meine Seele erhebt den Herrn*. Yet although there are some extraordinary, at times haunting, sounds in *Medusa*, Birtwistle never achieved the right proportions and he withdrew it, as he did most of the works he composed for the Pierrot Players.

*Verses for Ensembles*, on the other hand, was an unqualified success. Instead of a collection of heterogeneous instruments, the London Sinfonietta offered him three homogeneous groups: a percussion trio doubling tuned and untuned instruments, a woodwind quintet doubling high and low instruments, and a brass quintet. Once again, as in the other *Verses*, the platform on

---

* D'Arcy Thompson, *On Growth and Form*, abridged edition (Cambridge University Press, 1961), p. 13.

which they are situated is considered a stage, but here, instead of leaving the movement to the imagination of the audience, Birtwistle has the players move physically from position to position. At the back are two stands for the trumpets to play fanfares. In front of them are rows for tuned percussion, untuned percussion and brass. Still nearer the front and at right angles to them are what look like choir stalls for the woodwind, which at the very front (to continue in the ecclesiastic vein) are two lecterns for any instrumentalist who has a solo. The ecclesiastic allusion is not without justification, for as soon as the music starts it becomes evident that Birtwistle is making use of the two kinds of chant found in the Christian liturgy: antiphonal chant (the alternation of two or more choirs) and responsorial chant (the alternation of soloist and a single choir). There are twenty-six sections, grouped to conform to either one chant or the other, the whole giving the impression of an extremely formal ritual.

Yet when the sounds begin to impinge on the ear, one realizes it is not a Christian ritual but the desecration of one. They have a violence which can only be called barbaric: 'raw' is the word used in the score. Birtwistle says he composed the piece with the bit between his teeth: he was absolutely determined to make the most forthright and unequivocal statement he could deliver. As a result the work turned out to be a latter-day *Rite of Spring*. It is as stark and immutable as granite.

*Medusa* and *Verses for Ensembles* are rare specimens of Birtwistle's use of external referents. In his theatrical pieces, of course, they are essential, but on the whole he avoids them in other works simply because the dramas he enacts are internal rather than external. They are dramas of the mind and do not require external referents. In effect, they are projections of an internalized conflict which probably besets all children from a cohesive working-class community who consider themselves outsiders, the conflict between the necessity for individual self-assertion and the equally strong pull of the group. Expressed in Jungian terms (and Birtwistle's indebtedness to Jung is manifest, as we shall see) it involves the relationship between the ego, the centre of the conscious mind, and that deep layer of the unconscious mind Jung called the collective unconscious. This, he claimed, 'is self-identical in all Western men, and constitutes a psychic foundation, superpersonal in its nature, that is present in every one of us'.* It is that boundless, mysterious area from which consciousness has emerged and to which it must always refer. In all his music Birtwistle requires a soloist to represent the ego and chorus to represent the collective unconscious. When, for instance, he arranged the four solo instrumental movements in *Monodrama* as *Four Interludes from a Tragedy* (24) for basset clarinet, he was obliged to add synthesized sounds recorded on tape in order to create the illusion of a chorus always mysteriously there in the background. And even though *Monodrama* itself is a piece for a single soloist, as the title indicates, Birtwistle has the voice of Choregos, leader of the chorus, mysteriously projected over loudspeakers.

That he deals with internal processes is manifestly clear in *Cantata* (28), virtually the only piece written for the Pierrot Players which has not been withdrawn. The text consists of fragments taken from tombstone inscriptions and translations from Sappho and various editions of *The Greek Anthology*. Each is complete in itself, but although they obviously trace the cycle of a day, yawning connective gaps lie between them:

> Let all the earth shed tears... I begin with words of air yet they are good to hear... In gold sandals dawn like a thief falls upon me... Like the hyacinth there is a light blinding my eyes... Now in my heart I see clearly a beautiful face shining etched by love... Night closed my eyes and then poured down black sleep upon my lids... No longer will my mouth utter sounds nor clapping of hands follow.

The ambiguity of this sequence leaves it open to a host of interpretations, a feature which according to William Empson in *Seven Types of Ambiguity* is 'the essential fact about the poetical use of language';† but the discontinuities are also like those of inner speech, the speech one utters to oneself rather than to

---

* Carl J. Jung, *The Integration of the Personality* (Routledge and Kegan Paul, 1940), p. 53.
† William Empson, *Seven Types of Ambiguity* (Chatto and Windus, 1973), p. 25.

others. In inner speech connections are unnecessary because the context is understood. Often its syntax may only consist of predicates. Lev Vygotsky, in his classic essay on the subject, called inner speech 'a dynamic, shifting, unstable thing, fluttering between word and thought'.*

This could well be a description of the instrumental refrain which opens the work and frames the singer's verses. To establish the flickering effect of inner processes and to symbolize the amorphous nature of the collective unconscious, Birtwistle makes this refrain fluctuate considerably. Each of the five instruments (flute, clarinet, glockenspiel, violin and cello) has overlapping patterns and the players can choose how to perform them. This, for example, is the flute's part:

The player can select either the upper or lower traces with the omissions or alternatives indicated by the diagonal connecting lines. It is the conductor who chooses overall tempo, the duration of each separate beat, who decides whether the traces are to be played legato, detached or staccato, and whether dynamics A or B are to be played. Clearly no two realizations are likely to be the same: Birtwistle has invented for himself an almost inexhaustible pool of resources, and it is from this he draws the material for the verses.

*Lev Vygotsky, *Thought and Language* (MIT Press, Cambridge, Mass., 1962), p. 149.

He cites *Cantata* as a prime example of his use of interlocking techniques. In order to expand a simple three-note phrase such as his basic melodic cell of which the flute has three overlapping variants, he locks together several such cells so as to create a longer unit. But before illustrating the technique with a passage from the first verse, a frequently employed coordinating procedure he uses needs to be introduced. With it he relates one phrase to another by estimating the degree of rise or fall each contains. To estimate the relative amount of ascent or descent in a phrase, he gives a rise or fall between adjacent notes a count of one, between notes two semitones apart a count of two, between those three apart three, and so on. He then adds the numbers of ascents and descents in each phrase to produce a ratio. The six possible arrangements of the notes E F D sharp (his basic melodic cell) produce only four ratios, consequently phrases two and three can be deemed to be equivalent, as can phrases five and six.

In selecting five three-note phrases from the refrain in order to set the word 'tears', he was guided by the consideration that, although each phrase was different in intervallic content they could be coordinated in terms of shape. As the ratios indicate, the last two are the inverse of the first two, while the central one acts as a fulcrum and compensating balance for the phrase as a whole.

Birtwistle now interlocks these three-note phrases to produce a fairly complex line which, in a sense, flutters from one phrase to another. The density of interlockings is more complex at the centre of the line than at the fringes.

In making music out of this line, he alters the last two notes of the central phrase from E flat and F sharp to E natural and G to involve all twelve notes of the chromatic scale. The rhythm, nearly always just before or just after the implicit pulse, renders the line pliable and expressive.

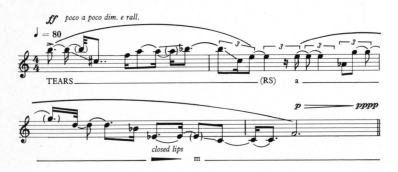

Were one to stand back and view all Birtwistle's work in perspective, its introspective quality would be more apparent than even such a piece as *Cantata* could reveal. At one level it reflects the flickering, unstable nature of mind itself, forever going back over things, forever relating past to present. At another it makes use of discontinuities, it assumes the context is understood and that connecting tissues are self-evident. At yet another it personifies traits of character (such as steadfastness and waywardness). In a wider sense it dramatizes the relationship between ego and the collective unconscious. Consequently, it might be said that all his music, whether theatrical, vocal or instrumental, is allegorical. It uses forms, textures, instrumentations, characters and events to symbolize moral, spiritual or psychological issues. His texts are either drawn from allegorical literature or are used for allegorical purpose. The only way to make sense of the text of *Cantata* is to interpret it as spiritual allegory. *Monody for Corpus Christi* (2), *Narration: A Description of the Passing of a Year* (8) and *Carmen Paschale* (13) are spiritual allegories too. And yet there is only one work Birtwistle actually subtitled an 'Allegory', *The Visions of Francesco Petrarca* (17), the splendid piece he wrote in 1966 for schoolchildren in York but unfortunately withdrew. The text is Edmund Spenser's translations of seven sonnets by Petrarch. Six of them describe an incident in which something beautiful—a hind, a tall ship, a laurel bush, a waterfall, a phoenix, a fair lady—is savagely destroyed in some way. A singer goes through each incident in song, then the children, accompanied by a school orchestra, retell them in dance. In the seventh sonnet all join together to deliver the spiritual homily:

> And though ye be the fairest of God's creatures,
> Yet think, that Death shall spoil your godly features.

The problem with allegory, particularly psychological allegory dealing with character traits or with problems of integration or individuation, is its tendency to be abstract. This is the problem that besets *Monodrama*. To be convincing, allegory needs a location, personifications and a plot which relate to real life, and these *Monodrama* does not possess. The location (in front of a portal) is vague; the personifications (protagonist, herald, prophetess and Choregos—who is never seen, are stereotypes; the plot almost non-existent. In *Punch and Judy* and all his subsequent theatre pieces, Birtwistle selects contexts which have the weight of tradition behind them. Mr Punch may be only a puppet, but he has enough human foibles to elicit laughter and sympathy.

Both *Monodrama* and *Punch and Judy* are designated 'source' works by Birtwistle. As mentioned already, this rather strange notion derives partly from the influence of Stravinsky, whose capacity to invent 'archaic worlds' he so much admires, and partly from his perpetual desire to turn back to the beginning, as every piece he has written demonstrates. *Punch and Judy* is meant to be the prototype opera. Stephen Pruslin says it is an opera about opera.

> It is an opera in quotation marks. The characters are stock-characters raised to a principle. The set-pieces ('quartet', 'love-duet', etc.) are likewise formulas that recur with different meanings in many operas. Our aim was the collective generalization of known operas into a 'source-opera' which, though written after them, would give the illusion of having been written before them.*

The idea succeeds in *Punch and Judy* because the various categories of opera are palpably obvious. It is heroic, romantic, picaresque, comic and tragic opera rolled into one. *Monodrama*, on the other hand, is not only abstract; the assumption upon which it is based, an assumption about the source of Greek tragedy, although of great significance to Birtwistle, is both relatively unfamiliar and factually suspect. Nevertheless, it is also central to *Punch and Judy*, the major work of this period, and must be discussed.

It is the idea put forward by Nietzsche in *The Birth of Tragedy*, and claims that tragedy deals with the conflict and ultimate reconciliation of Apollonian individualism, as embodied in the protagonist, and Dionysian universalism, as embodied in the chorus: 'the chorus remains the highest expression of nature', Nietzsche said, 'and, like nature, utters in its enthusiasm oracular words of wisdom. Being compassionate as well as wise, it proclaims a truth that issues from the heart of the world.'† It was the genius of the classical Greek spirit to recognize these polarities and to effect a balance between them in drama. Once the relationship was severed, as it was after the death of Euripides, when the chorus was virtually eliminated, the

---

* Sleevenote for Decca recording.
† Friedrich Nietzsche, *The Birth of Tragedy* (Doubleday Anchor, 1956), p. 57.

spiritual balance, celebrated by tragedy, was destroyed. Individualism lost its moorings and was adrift.

This assumption not only fits Birtwistle's *modus operandi*, it is also in accord with Jungian psychology. The balance between ego and the collective unconscious results in that unity of personality Jung calls the 'self'. When this is out of balance, the personality loses its integrity. The nub of Jung's theory is that ego and collective unconscious are mutually compensatory. If one is strong, the other is weak; if Mr Punch's ego becomes too assertive it will overwhelm Choregos, the chorus, the collective. To restore the balance Punch must recognize the situation and make amends. It is perhaps significant in respect to Jungian psychology that the recognition comes in the form of a dream, or rather, a nightmare.

Choregos is the only character in *Punch and Judy* who is not a puppet. As showman and compere he runs the show. In *Monodrama* he is merely a voice over the loudspeaker system. This has the effect of drawing the audience into the solipsistic environment; the whole theatre becomes mind, physically; like the set in Beckett's *Endgame*, it represents a skull. Behind the portal, we are told, someone has screamed: 'a scream is the portal of pain'. To discover who it was and why it happened, the voice of Choregos persuades the protagonist to consult first a herald, the personification of reason, and then a prophetess. (In the manner of an early form of Greek theatre all roles are played by the same person: hence the title of the work.) Neither can help, but upon the prophetess's repeated cry 'facts chime doom', which alludes to the self-destructive assertiveness of the ego, the protagonist herself screams. She now recognizes the truth. The victim and the slayer were none other than herself. (The motto selected to head the libretto of *Punch and Judy* is Sophocles' 'Who is the slayer, who is the victim? Speak'). Having discovered this, she too can make amends. The work ends with the protagonist embroidering Choregos' words in ever more elaborate melismatic phrases—music blossoming out of speech, as it were—then dying away to a pianissimo close.

It is very impressive and the work contains other imaginative felicities, but because it posseses little dramatic tension the catastrophe seems incidental rather than integral. What is even more surprising from Birtwistle is that the continuity is almost linear. The encounters with the herald and with the prophetess go through the same routine without any formal deviations. He seems to be avoiding discursiveness, avoiding the impression that we are witnessing the thinking process itself. Instead we have a structure at odds with the plot.

It was composed during his first year in America at Princeton. Perhaps even then the Schenkerian method which emphasizes the paramount importance of linear continuity* and is so pervasive in America, was beginning to affect him. Certainly when he went to Boulder to study Schenkerianism, he seemed entirely under its sway, for it was there that he composed *Nomos* (22), the orchestral piece commissioned for the 1968 Promenade Concerts. Once again the title, a Greek word, has wide implications. It refers to both the melodic patterns which accompanied the recitation of the epics and concepts of law and order. Like many of his large-scale works it has cycles within cycles. In this case, three large cycles contain nine short cycles, each subject to invented laws of expansion and contraction. This, for Birtwistle, is standard practice. What is unusual is that throughout the piece four amplified wind instruments, flute, clarinet, horn and bassoon, unfold very slowly a long *cantus firmus*, which for all intents and purposes is through-composed. In true Schenkerian fashion it represents a prolongation of a melodic movement from the dominant (G) to the tonic (C). Also unusual is the shift of emphasis in the relation between solo and chorus. Normally the last word is given to the chorus. Here the four amplified instruments as soloists and the orchestra as chorus reverse this procedure. At first the orchestra dominates, but as the work proceeds the amplified quartet becomes louder and more active until eventually it silences the orchestra and ultimately itself in a flurry of assertiveness.

---

* Schenker, who analysed only classical masters from Bach to Brahms, believed that in their music melody, harmony and rhythm had their source in a basic line which at its deepest level is simply a three-note progression from the third to the first degree of the scale. Tracing the linear continuity which arose from this was the essence of his method.

It is a strange piece. Perhaps a clue to what was intended can be obtained from the next piece he composed, a piece also concerned with continuous line: *Linoi* (23). Here the soloist is a basset clarinet in A, and the chorus notes plucked from inside a grand piano. Linoi were lamentations originally sung for Linus, the young musician who, according to tradition, brought about his own destruction by daring to challenge the musical authority of Apollo. The piece has been described as 'the generation, the simultaneous flowering and destruction, and the prolonged death agony of a single melodic line'. Although built on the usual principle of alternations between chorus and verse ending with a reversal of this ordering, the clarinet line, like the line in *Nomos*, never stops. It rises in a series of mounting undulations during which it becomes ever-increasingly fractured until a hair-raising climax is reached. But its efforts, like the efforts of Linus, have brought about its own destruction and it sinks to its lowest note *a niente*.

Birtwistle himself provided the moral for these two sad tales, or at least Ockeghem did in the instrumental motet Birtwistle arranged for the Pierrot Players in 1969: *Ut Heremita Solus* (29). In this the *cantus firmus*, given twice, becomes increasingly splintered, and dissociated from the free upper and lower voices, which act as chorus to its solo. On the second occurrence its character is drastically altered by rhythmic diminution. The text associated with the *cantus firmus* is, 'As a hermit I wait alone until my mutation comes.' In other words, individual solo lines which go their own sweet way or silence the supporting chorus destroy themselves. Birtwistle insists, in this period, that the individual cannot survive without the collective, without 'the other'. The outrageously assertive Punch needs to be tempered by Choregos, his social and psychological complement, and by Pretty Poll, his ideal woman and spiritual complement.

As an aside, it may be worth mentioning that in his next period, when he embarks on the all-consuming Orpheus legend, the relationship between the individual and the collective alters. Orpheus does not separate himself from others out of self-assertion, but out of introspection. It is not the ego which overwhelms the collective, it is the collective which overwhelms the ego. Orpheus is torn to pieces by the Maenads because, in devoting himself entirely to the memory of Euridice, he neglects them. And yet it is not the Maenads who survive, it is Orpheus. It is he who is remembered and celebrated in poem after poem, opera after opera. In this next period of Birtwistle's development, his newly-found confidence, after the debacle with the Pierrot Players, is mirrored by a shift to the primacy of the individual.

In the period of *Punch and Judy*, however, he is still focused on the balance between individual and chorus. *Punch and Judy* is a complex work, not only because it attempts to be a 'source-opera', but because to include the relationship between individual and chorus, and to effect a balance between them, Birtwistle has to introduce elements not normally included in the traditional show of seaside, fêtes and fairs. In any case, the traditional show is not structured enough, it is too much an aggregate consisting of a series of almost identical incidents: Punch throwing baby out of the window, beating and killing Judy, a Doctor and various other characters, cheating the hangman into hanging himself and then disposing of the devil. To give it coherence he treats these incidents as a moral allegory and locks into them the psychological allegory of Punch and Choregos, and the spiritual allegory of Punch and Pretty Poll. Behind these lie three quite different literary traditions: medieval morality play (of which *Everyman* is the most celebrated), Greek tragedy and Arthurian Romance (the quests for Pretty Poll are undertaken to find spiritual redemption).

Punch, who is closely related to Pulcinella, actually has his roots in Italy. He first made his appearance in Naples during the sixteenth century, dressed, says Enid Welsford in her book on the fool, 'in a wide blouse and pantaloons, with a conical hat on his head, a black half-mask over his protuberant hooked nose, and an ominous cudgel in his hand'.* He was one of a group of 'subnormal men who please by the exhibition of stupidity and

---

* Enid Welsford, *The Fool, his Social and Literary History* (Faber and Faber, 1935), pp. 300–1.

insensibility'. When Italian actors and puppeteers flocked to Britain with the re-opening of theatres at the Restoration, Punch came with them. As a puppet he was grafted on to the vestige of the old allegorical morality play which still lingered on, taking over the role of Old Vice, the outrageous buffoon who encapsulated all the vices of the other characters. In the Italian tradition of the Harlequinade the action terminated with Punch or Pulcinella hanging the hangman; in the English tradition it terminated with the defeat of the devil, not by Old Vice, but by the most virtuous character on stage—Everyman perhaps.

The hangman (Jack Ketch, the notorious public executioner between 1663 and 1686) and the devil are combined in the opera, and it is the hanging of him which makes Punch virtuous enough to be accepted by Pretty Poll. Pretty Poll was one of the characters who appeared when the puppet show was reshaped at the beginning of the nineteenth century. Unlike the other characters, which are hand-puppets, she was a doll on a stick. Later she disappeared, but at no time in the traditional show was she ever the object of a quest. In the opera Punch sets out to find her, like some knight-errant on his hobby-horse, three times, but each time he finds her she rejects him because of the crimes he has committed. Only when the devil within him is vanquished does she relent. In the final apotheosis, as all dance round a maypole with one of the dancers dressed as the traditional Green Man, everyone joins in the chorus: 'Man and wife, wife and man together complete the celestial plan'. The Green Man, the personification of nature, also appears in the great fourteenth-century romance, *Sir Gawain and the Green Knight*. Birtwistle had set a passage of this poem in *Narration: A Description of the Passing of a Year* (8) some six months before embarking on the opera, and it was still very much on his mind. Sir Gawain also goes on a quest and he too is tested three times by a lady. At the end of the poem when Sir Gawain has proved his 'good faith', what is achieved, says John Speirs*

---

* John Speirs, 'A Survey of Medieval Verse and Drama' in *The New Pelican Guide to English Literature*, Vol. 1 (Penguin, 1982), p. 62.

seems to be a kind of adjustment, if not reconciliation, between man and nature, between the human and the other than human. In a limited sense, the courtly order has been put to the test of nature. As a consequence Gawain recognises his own nature, knows himself.

This by implication, is what Punch recognizes too.

*Sir Gawain and the Green Knight* is an alliterative poem, and this technique clearly influenced Stephen Pruslin in his libretti for both *Punch and Judy* and *Monodrama*, indeed the use of alliteration and of assonance in these libretti reflects a concern for the sounds of words apparent in the work of all those who provide texts for Birtwistle. On paper or in speech both appear very contrived, but in music they can crystallize the attitude or emotion the singer has to impart very effectively, as Wagner knew to his advantage. In addition, they allow Pruslin to slide into the childish puns and riddle games, so appropriate for Punch, as if they were a natural mode of behaviour.

The *dramatis personae* are Punch, Judy (later a Fortune-teller), Choregos (later Jack Ketch), Pretty Poll (later a Witch), Doctor and Lawyer, with five mime-dancers who act as a silent chorus in order to intensify certain climatic moments of the drama. The murders being ritual, those killed appear again, take on other roles and join in the singing chorus. Performed without a break, the piece is cast as a series of melodramas and quests interrupted by a nightmare after the murder of Choregos. In a prologue, Choregos welcomes the audience to the 'littel play', and the curtain rises on Punch serenading baby, who is thrown not out of the window but into the fire (Birtwistle has never forgotten the opening sequence of the first film he saw as a boy, the shots of babies being thrown into a fire at the start of Eisenstein's *Alexander Nevsky*). Judy enters and after accusing him she too is killed. Punch then goes on his first quest for Pretty Poll who dismisses the flower he offers her imperiously: 'The flaw in this flower is a flicker of flame.' In the following melodrama Punch encounters Doctor and Lawyer, killing one with a hypodermic syringe, the other with a quill. Pretty Poll rejects him again. Punch returns home to confront Choregos, who perishes in the bass viol case amid an orgy of *Gebrauchsmusik* (utility music associated with Hindemith). After that the quest takes Punch northward 'to the land of infinite night'. In his nightmare on the journey his victims turn against him; Judy is a fortune-teller with a wicked pack of tarot cards, Pretty Poll a witch. When he awakens in terror to continue his journey, Pretty Poll's pedestal is deserted. In the last melodrama Punch is in prison awaiting the hangman whom he cheats into hanging himself: 'Huzzah, huzzah! the Devil's dead!' he cries. Pretty Poll comes to life; they sing a love-duet, the gallows is transformed into a maypole, and in an epilogue Choregos bids the audience farewell.

Everything about the piece—set, lighting, acting, singing—is meant to be as artificial and as stylized as possible. The music is equally stylized. It is modelled on that which was itself highly stylized—the baroque. But because baroque opera was never tragic nor made as extensive use of the chorus as Birtwistle required (not even *tragédie lyrique*), the specific model is not an opera, but the *St Matthew Passion*. Like Bach's masterpiece, *Punch and Judy* abounds in Chorales, of which three are Passion Chorales, while the most poignant moment is undoubtedly the second Passion Aria which Judy sings after Choregos has been ushered into the bass viol case; an extended da capo aria with oboe d'amore obbligato to the words 'Be silent, strings of my heart. The rainbow on this bridge reveals suspensions of eternal harmony.' Choregos, in the way he comments on and links the various episodes, is both chorus and evangelist, a role emphasized by the expressive, *parlando* style of his delivery.

Nevertheless, tragedy, or rather the possibility of tragedy, is only one aspect of the work. In the end it reverts to being a morality, and is therefore not so different from baroque opera after all. Like baroque opera, it is a number opera—in fact, the number opera *par excellence*. There are well over a hundred separate items, some like the Toccatas which frame the Passion Chorales lasting only a few seconds. All, however, conform to the baroque doctrine of *Affectenlehre* in that each encapsulates a specific attitude or response which can be morally assessed. The Toccatas, for instance, are meant to sound 'like some mechanical process switched on and off' so that the Passion

65

Chorales seem to be an automatic rather than a spontaneous response. But the most memorable 'affect', the one that could be heard whistled in the streets of Aldeburgh after the first performance, is the self-satisfied gavotte Punch sings whenever he has killed someone.

Many of the longer numbers are also couched in baroque forms, such as the ternary Passion Aria and the binary gavotte, but mostly they are either song or answering forms. The latter are particularly prevalent in the melodramas and indeed are the special feature of them. They are the question-and-answer games children play in order to eliminate someone: 'Answer me this or out you go'. With Judy Punch plays a word-game, with Doctor and Lawyer a riddle-game and with Jack Ketch an interview game. He always wins, of course, except when the tables are turned on him in the nightmare.

The structure of the melodramas varies according to which person is being tested, but they are always in two parts and always contain the following events: Punch's encounter with the victim, who establishes the principle he or she represents; the question-and-answer game, then a murder ensemble consisting of a proclamation from Choregos about the arrogance of Punch, 'that high priest of pain', couplets on the bitter sweetness of death, the murder, and Punch's resolve (the gavotte) to search for Pretty Poll.

The quests, on the other hand, are absolutely regular, except when Punch finds the pedestal deserted. Travel music is followed by a weather-report from the chorus, an extremely moving prayer for the chorus and Choregos, Punch's serenade and Poll's rhapsodic dismissal. The episode ends with the most expressive music in the whole opera, music not unlike that given to the Evangelist when reporting Peter's denial in the *St Matthew Passion*. It is Choregos singing: 'Weep, my Punch. Weep out your unfathomable, inexpressible sorrow.'

These words also echo the final chorus of the *St Matthew Passion*, but there the tears of grief are mingled with thoughts of the resurrection. And so it is here. Not that Punch is Christ, but he is certainly a pagan fertility figure, who dies in winter when he finds Pretty Poll's pedestal empty and is reborn again 'as blazing sun to zenith speeds'. Each of his guests has been taken at a certain time, in a certain season, in a certain direction, under a certain sign. At the end all cycles are completed. 'Spring has come, shattering the prism, dispelling the eclipse, unfreezing the stars.'

Images of death and resurrection pervade Birtwistle's work. Just as his structures reflect cycles of recurrence, so do his texts. It is the one feature they all have in common. Nowhere is this so clearly in evidence than in *Down by the Greenwood Side* (27), the theatre piece described as a Dramatic Pastoral which he composed in collaboration with Michael Nyman in 1969 for the Brighton Festival. If *Punch and Judy* is based on the oldest surviving specimen of urban entertainment in Britain, this is based on the oldest surviving rural entertainment: the Mummers' Play, the traditional dumb-show which took place at Christmas yet celebrated the coming of spring. It is cast in the form known to folklorists as 'combat-and-cure', an allegory of fertility and spiritual regeneration. The master of ceremonies, Father Christmas, defines the area and ushers in the invincible champion, no less a person than St George himself, personfication of England, the land and its people, who issues a challenge. His evil opponent, Bold Slasher, the Saracen infidel, representative of the hardness of the frost-bound earth in winter, replies. They fight and St George dies. He is cured by a doctor. They fight again and again St George dies. This time the cure is effected by Jack Finney, who is none other than the Green Man. As soon as he appears, Bold Slasher leaves.

Nyman arranged the text from nineteenth-century versions of the play which was then spoken rather than mimed; and for the instrumentation of the piece Birtwistle turned to the nineteenth-century words of the Cornish Floral Dance: 'We danced to the band with the curious tone of cornet, clarinet and big trombone; fiddle, cello, big bass drum, flute, bassoon, euphonium.'

The Mummers' Play is spoken and constitutes the comic element in the Pastoral. The serious element, which is strategically interlocked with it, is the macabre ballad of the Cruel Mother, who on this occasion is called Mrs Green after the most modern version which Nyman places at the end. Most versions of the ballad came from Scotland, of which the earliest recorded dates from 1776. Variants can also be found in England and as far away as Denmark and Germany. The details vary considerably, but the gist remains the same. A young girl has a love affair with her father's clerk. In the heart of a forest, down by the greenwood side, she gives birth to twin boys whom she kills out of shame. Years later she sees two pretty boys playing in the forest. They are naked so she tells them that were they hers she would care for them and dress them in fineries. 'When we were thine,' they answer, 'you dressed us in your own heart's blood.'

Three versions of this are interpolated into the Mummers' Play. One begins the action and is completed after the first death of St George, the next occurs after the second death, while the third, the most recent version which ends with Mrs Green being packed off to prison, is completed by Father Christmas. For the first and only time, Mrs Green momentarily enters the Mummers' acting area.

Once again Birtwistle has written an allegory on various levels and once again a soloist (Mrs Green) has been pitted against a chorus (the Mummers). But until the end the two have been separate from each other. What characterizes Mrs Green is her self-absorption which so irritates the Mummers that they call the police to drag her off. *Down by the Greenwood Side* marks the end of a period of intense dramatic and theatrical activity, but it also heralds the switch in focus mentioned earlier, a switch encapsulated in the legend of Orpheus.

# 5:  SEVEN PROCESSIONALS

THE IDEA OF SETTING a text about the death of Orpheus had originally been suggested by pupils at Cranborne Chase School. They thought Birtwistle, with his taste for unusual contexts, would be intrigued that in Virgil's *Georgics* the episode is introduced to warn beekeepers that if they offended common decency their swarms would disappear. When in 1970 Dinah Casson, one of those pupils, and her fiancé Nick Wood asked him to write something for their wedding reception, he was reminded of the Orpheus episode, but in the event the piece he wrote, *Nenia: The Death of Orpheus* (34), was given to the soprano Jane Manning for the newly-formed Matrix (soprano, three clarinets, piano and percussion), while Dinah and Nick were presented with a love song not directly connected with the Orpheus legend but certainly associated with it.

Barely had he completed these when an invitation came to write an opera: inevitably the subject he chose was Orpheus whom Julian Budden calls 'the godparent of opera'. He continues:

> He is there at its birth and he tends to return at crises in its history, when the genre itself seems to be due for reappraisal. If you want to pioneer a new theory of opera, Orpheus is the usual subject with which to do it ... So Peri and Caccini, aiming at a modern equivalent of Greek tragedy, chose the legend with which to launch the new

genre about 1600. Monteverdi, less doctrinaire but equally an innovator, did the same. One hundred and fifty years later Gluck, in his aim of redressing the balance between music and drama, turned again to Orpheus.*

Birtwistle follows in their footsteps, for there can be no doubt that *The Mask of Orpheus* (60) is also intended as an act of reappraisal.

The basic story has come down to us from Roman rather than Greek sources. Details vary, but the main ingredients are constant. Shortly after her marriage to Orpheus, Euridice is walking by a river when she excites the passion of the beekeeper Aristaeus who pursues her through the long grass. In her flight she fails to notice a poisonous snake, and is killed. So great is the grief of her husband that he determines to retrieve her from Hades. There he charms Charon and the powers of darkness with his singing and is able to cross the river Styx. His song moves even Pluto, who allows him to take Euridice back to earth on condition he does not look back at her; but he does, and loses her a second time. He then renounces women and sings only to trees and rocks. This eventually arouses the fury of the Maenads (female followers of Dionysus) who tear him apart, casting his still murmuring head and lyre on the river Hebrus. From there they float to Lesbos where, on the intervention of Apollo, his ghost passes beneath the earth to join Euridice according to the usual ordinance.

The contrast between the power of music and the frailty of the musician makes this story particularly appealing to musicians. Through his art the musician can control the emotions of others even if he cannot control his own. This is firmly established in the first musical treatment of the story, that of Angelo Poliziano's *La Fabula d'Orfeo* (1480), which could well lay claim to being the first opera, even though it lacked issue and none of its music survives. The three main topics—Aristaeus' passion, Orpheus' grief and the Maenads' fury—drive home the Platonic

---

*Julian Budden, 'Orpheus, or the Sound of Music', *Opera*, August 1967, p. 623.

thesis that excess of emotion leads to disaster. Peri and Caccini, on the other hand, focus on another aspect. Pluto imposes no condition upon Orpheus and the couple return united. What they stress is the new humanist philosophy that the purpose of music is not to perfect the intellect (as medieval opinion held), but to stimulate the passions. This was also Monteverdi's intention, yet by including the second death of Euridice he gives the story a Platonic slant again. In the eighteenth-century Haydn's opera *L'Anima del Filosofo* (1791) continues the Platonic vein. The philosopher of the title is not Orpheus but Creonte, Euridice's father. According to him, 'our emotions are tyrants and yet we boast of liberty'.

Thirty years earlier Gluck's well-known *Orfeo ed Euridice* cast a new light on the legend. The power of music is still central; what changes is the nature of the musician's frailty. Orpheus becomes the epitome of restraint rather than impetuosity. In embodying what Gluck's contemporary Winkelmann called 'noble simplicity and quiet grandeur', Orpheus strives not for physical gratification but spiritual perfection. It is Euridice who wants physical gratification. As she follows him out of Hades she tells Orpheus that if he will neither touch nor look at her she might as well return whence she came. Suddenly Orpheus can no longer maintain his restraint and quite out of character turns. *Che faro* may be as poised and controlled as anything he has sung before, but that moment of impulse gives it additional poignancy. Immediately afterwards he begs to die himself. This is the *peripeteia*. He has accepted the limitation of spiritual aspiration and Jupiter is prepared to forgive him.

Since then, Apollonian restraint has been the most emphasized feature of musical versions. It is this which Offenbach satirizes, and in Stravinsky's ballet, which must be the most chaste score he ever wrote, Orpheus is so controlled that when he tears the bandage from his eyes to look at Euridice it appears an act of defiance rather than impulse. At the end Stravinsky makes explicit what was perhaps only implicit in Gluck, for the climax is the apotheosis of Orpheus as God of Song. As a man he must acknowledge his mortality, but as a musician, as a creator of songs, he has at last transcended death.

71

Birtwistle takes all these versions into account and many others as well. Characteristically, he looks at the story from as many angles as possible in order to produce an extremely dense amalgam. He incorporates Jung's ideas about Orpheus and as much as is known about Orphism, the mystery religion widespread through ancient Greece. Basically, this involved abstinence and the transmigration of souls, although Arthur Koestler speculated that it was equally concerned with the mathematical aspect of the mysteries of nature. The word 'theory', he says, is of Orphic origin and means a state of fervent contemplation:

> Contemplation of the 'divine dance of numbers' which held both the secrets of music and of the celestial motions became the link in the mystic union between human thought and the *anima mundi*. Its perfect symbol was the Harmony of the Spheres—the Pythagorean scale, whose musical intervals corresponded to the intervals between the planetary orbits.*

For a musician so indebted to numbers as Birtwistle, such speculation inevitably influences *The Mask of Orpheus*. But the opera has had a protracted history. Sixteen years separate the original commission in 1970 to the intended debut in 1986 at the Coliseum in London. During this time the commission has passed from Covent Garden to London Weekend Television to Glyndebourne and now to the only other opera company with resources to mount it, English National Opera. Undoubtedly Birtwistle's reappraisal of the genre is so extreme that the task of mounting it has been daunting. Certainly a director of genius is required to realize Birtwistle and Zinovieff's intentions.

If *Punch and Judy* with its abrupt juxtapositions, its rapid cutting and freezing, is an extreme example of the Theatre of Cruelty, *The Mask of Orpheus* takes Antonin Artaud's precepts several stages further. Later, when the opera is discussed in

* Arthur Koestler, *The Act of Creation* (Pan, 1970), p. 262.

detail, the extent of the influence will become evident; suffice it to say now that the paraphernalia includes the most elaborate stage mechanisms, taped inserts and a quite extraordinary orchestra. In addition, each of the main characters, Orpheus, Euridice and Aristaeus (whom Birtwistle calls 'the shadow') appears as singer, mime and huge puppet. It is no wonder that the major companies balked.

The first two acts were composed between 1973 and 1975 when Birtwistle was in the United States teaching first at Swarthmore College, Pennsylvania, and then, on the invitation of his friend Morton Feldman, at New York State University at Buffalo. On his return to take up his appointment at the National Theatre, Glyndebourne had thoughts of mounting the opera but they never materialized, so the third act was left in abeyance. Thus it remained until the early eighties when English National Opera took over the responsibilty and with their firm promise of a production Birtwistle completed it.

During these years some twenty-five other pieces have been composed, all, in one way or another, influenced by the opera. In fact, with *Nenia*, the first of them, came a change of style, or at least a change of mood. Gone were the symmetries, the hard edges, the abrupt juxtapositions; in their place comes a darker more sensuous tone. Discussing this change in the sleeve-note for the gramophone record of *Verses for Ensembles* and *Nenia*, Michael Nyman called it a primarily melodic, non-dynamic, processional style:

> Now colours and densities evolve and change gradually as in a procession across a landscape, and time is not sharply subdivided (as it is in *Verses*) but unfolds as a broad, slowly-progressing continuum.

He then goes on to quote an important and extremely pertinent statement from the composer himself:

> Of time, music's most precious commodity, Birtwistle has recently said: 'Music is the one medium where time can transcend itself more than anything else. With poetry you

73

are always up against language and meaning—in theatre too—while with painting you're up against the frame, which limits the size and scale. Time scale in music is something which has nothing to do with the length of a piece—and new concepts of time are my main compositional preoccupation.

Time, as we have seen, is one of the essential ingedients of the Orpheus legend. All versions include the desire to reverse time, to return to a time when Euridice was still alive. Hence the condition imposed upon Orpheus: he must not look back. Pluto is prepared to reverse time provided Orpheus is not party to the subterfuge, provided he continues to look ahead.

This, of course, is analogous with Birtwistle's compositional methods: when he turns back to begin a new cycle, time is reversed; yet in moving towards a *peripeteia* he keeps his eyes firmly ahead. The two processes complement each other. What he now requires is a third temporal dimension to complete the frame, the dimension in which time is transcended. For this, the legend of Orpheus offers great opportunities.

Similar opportunities can be derived from the form known as 'the processional'. Of the twenty-five pieces composed during these fourteen years, more than half come into this category. Their purpose is to convey the impression of walking through a landscape, or perhaps, as in the case of *The Triumph of Time*, of watching a parade. Four of the seven composed between 1970 and 1973, *Nenia, Dinah and Nick's Love Song, Meridian, The Fields of Sorrow*, are closely related to Orpheus, while the other three, *The Triumph of Time, An Imaginary Landscape* and *Grimethorpe Aria*, although seemingly independent of it, share the same preoccupations. A central feature of all these pieces is the development of time transcended. Birtwistle explores various possibilities, but he finds the most appropriate way to express it is through an aria.

But what, it may be asked, have new concepts of time to do with walking through a landscape? The answer is that we are so used to measuring things in terms of clock time, that we forget that time is multi-dimensional; things change at different rates.

According to Einstein what we call time is not one velocity but a coordination of many. We notice this only when faced with it graphically, when walking through a landscape perhaps. It is then that temporal perspective become synonymous with visual perspective. Events close at hand appear to be moving more rapidly than those in the distance simply because we can see them more clearly. Perhaps it is only when we look at a mountain range or the stars at night that we have a sense of time-lessness.

Distance in music can be conveyed in three ways: the most obvious is simply to distance the musicians physically; another is to layer or counterpoint different rates of change; yet another is to distort, blur or reflect sound as happens in nature. Gabrieli, in St Mark's, depended upon distributing his musicians spatially; later composers such as Ives, Vaughan Williams and Holst, all of whom produced some fine processionals, relied upon layering different rates of change—Holst's *Egdon Heath*, for instance, creates an impression of walking through a landscape by means of superimposing and interlocking various velocities, the whole being underpinned by gentle marching rhythm. With the advent of Stockhausen's *Gruppen* for three orchestras, composers have become much more aware of the possibilities offered by distortion, blurring and reflection.

In opera distance was traditionally created by echo effects. Nowhere have these been more in evidence than in the operas dealing with Orpheus. When Orpheus' voice is echoed in the first act of Gluck's opera, the effect is of a vast empty space, a space devoid of Euridice. In Monteverdi's opera echoes suggest the boundless space of Hades. Indeed, the journey through Hades takes place musically even as Orpheus speaks to Charon, for it is then that the echoes of violin, cornetto and harp are heard as a backcloth to the great lament: *Possente spirito.*

The journey through Hades culminating in the procession of Orpheus and Euridice returning is the centrepiece of the story. *Nenia* (34) begins after it is over and ends with the head and lyre floating downstream. Nevertheless, the procession continues to reverberate in Orpheus' mind until the moment he is killed. 'Nenia' is Latin for a mournful song, in this instance the mournful song of a female singer accompanied by a flute at Orpheus' funeral.

On this occasion the instruments are three bass clarinets, a set of crotales (antique cymbals), a prepared piano and a piano played pizzicato. At the climax of the piece, though, the first clarinet changes to a soprano instrument and plays in a flute-like manner. The vocal part, being written for Jane Manning, is exceptionally virtuosic, for it incorporates the roles of narrator as well as Orpheus and Euridice all interlocked with each other. As narrator, she must use *Sprechgesang*; as Orpheus the melismatic, *fioriture* style associated with Monteverdi; while as Euridice the *bel canto* style associated with Gluck.

By dividing the vocal part in this way, three different time dimensions are suggested. The first is the time of the narrator relating the dry facts of the story. As an accompaniment to this, the instruments suggest the ominous tread of the Maenads in the distance, the tearing apart of Orpheus, and the floating of the head and lyre downstream. This is goal-orientated time. The second is the time of Orpheus looking back, 're-enacting the moment when he last saw her, hoping to *catch Euridice in time*'. The italics are not Peter Zinovieff's; they are added to draw attention to the comparable situation in music: trying to catch something in time is the principle activity of composers. So it is of Orpheus. There are two aspects of his looking back: going over the return journey again is one, the other is his attempt to articulate a song. In the event, though, it is Euridice who sings it on his behalf: 'What blame? What sin? That of having too much loved me? Orpheus, my love, love me still too much, love me, love me.'

The voice of Euridice singing 'Orpheus, my love' continues even as the first clarinet portrays the tearing apart. It constitutes the third temporal dimension, the time of Orpheus and Euridice calling to each other down the ages endlessly. Birtwistle places their calls in the interstices of the narrator's *Sprechgesang* so that the effect is achieved musically; nevertheless, the mere repetition of their names might have been enough to suggest timelessness.

Changeless repetition may suggest timelessness; it can also

76

suggest 'the triumph of time'. In the piece so named an unchanging saxophone phrase suddenly explodes into frenzied activity; in *Nenia* three bass clarinets, which clearly represent the chorus of Maenads, suddenly switch from inactivity to intense activity as soon as Euridice finishes her song. The Maenads have made their attack: time the destroyer triumphs.

Distance plays a part in this passage too. The relative lack of activity suggests something far away, as does the blurring of pitch and rhythm. Until the climax the three clarinets stay in their lowest registers; but when the attack comes the pitch of the first clarinet shifts to its highest register and the resultant clarity brings the sound leaping forward. No sooner is it over than Birtwistle devises 'mobiles', to create a floating quality for the head and lyre drifting downstream. The soprano clarinet, crotales and piano gently tolling single notes independently of each other make one mobile, while the two bass clarinets make another. Each has the same three phrases with specified differences in tempo and repetitions but unspecified differences in the order they are to appear. They float about each other haphazardly.

These two mobiles, one of related but independent pulses, the other of related but independent melodies, are also the basis of *Dinah and Nick's Love Song* (35). In this a harp has the pulse (plus a recurring cadence to punctuate the sections of the piece), while three identical melody instruments have the melodies. What is unusual about the piece is the harmonic relation between the harp and the melody instruments, for any three identical instruments can play regardless of whether they transpose or not. The pitch of the harp is always constant, but that of the melody instruments differs according to whether, say, cors anglais or soprano saxophones are playing. This might be considered an illustration of Birtwistle's indifference to pitch, but on closer inspection it suggests a perfect analogy to the marriage ceremony: 'for better for worse, for richer for poorer, in sickness and in health...' The essence of marriage is that the relationship can adapt itself to changing circumstances and this is exactly what happens here. The harp framing the work with repeated cadences provides all the necessary

77

harmonic stability required.

In a sense, *Dinah and Nick's Love Song* represents the quint-essential love song; perhaps it was the one Orpheus struggled to articulate but could not. Traditionally his songs are either laments or pleas for pity, rather than expressions of love. Indeed, a great deal of the interest in Orpheus stems from the fatal flaw in his love.

*Nenia*, in the tradition of the early operas, follows Ovid and Virgil in maintaining that Orpheus loved too much. Birtwistle might well have chosen the opposite opinion, that he loved too little. In *The Symposium* Plato has it that all true lovers are prepared to die for each other, but Orpheus

> lacked spirit, as is only natural in a musician; he had not the courage to die for love . . . but contrived to enter Hades alive. For this they punished him and caused him to meet his death at the hands of women.*

Another tradition has it that he lost Euridice because his love was too cerebral. This has been the dominant view since Gluck; it was held by Jung and is continued in *The Mask of Orpheus*. But once again there is a contrary opinion. In the Middle Ages, especially among those philosophers who were also musical theorists, notably Boethius (*c.* 480–524) and the Scot, Erigena (810–872), it was held that Orpheus' love was too physical. Birtwistle set Boethius' text about Orpheus in *On the Sheer Threshold of the Night* (57) which will be discussed in detail later. Its purport is that had he kept his eyes on the light of reason ahead of him all would have been well; but in turning to look back at Euridice in the twilight of unreason he lost her. Erigena shifts the emphasis by specifically relating the legend to the nature of music itself. He claimed there were three stages in the process of listening. The first is concerned with sensory stimulation, sound *per se*; the second draws in the formal structure, so that the sound has significance as well. The third

* Plato. *The Symposium*, trans. W. Hamilton (Penguin Classics, 1951), p. 44.

stage, however, involves listening with the mind alone. Here the listener plunges into a world of mystery, a world where the laws of harmony, primary proportions and eternal number hold sway:

> This feeling of mystery is expressed in allegorical form in the legend of Orpheus and Euridice. Orpheus is the symbol of that wondrous song which we apprehend through our ears in the physical world. Euridice is the image of the intelligible, divine mystery concealed in every melody. But once the sensibility attempts, through the activity of consciousness, to clarify the profound, absolute significance of the harmony, everything vanishes. At the very moment we believe we are hearing and under-standing, we find ourselves plunged back into the shadows, and we are forced to be content with the unresolved mystery.*

This is the central concern of *Meridian* (36). It is a setting of a love song by Christopher Logue from the collection *Wand and Quadrant* which Birtwistle had also plundered for *Ring a Dumb Carillon*. It compares the unchanging nature of 'the image of love', the rose, with the ephemerality of that 'dunce of birds', the cock, singing on the briar as if 'he knew the origin of flames that burn his thigh'. Yet, concludes the poem, his song 'is lie or nonsense'; the cock cannot penetrate the mystery and 'the rose grows on'.

Birtwistle frames this text with stanzas from two poems by Sir Thomas Wyatt, 'My lute awake', and 'Blame not my lute'. These not only provide an appropriate context, but also relate the work more closely to Orpheus. The word 'meridian' also has Orphean connections. In classical mythology the cock is dedicated to Apollo because it gives notice of the sun; classical mythology also claims that the sun is Orpheus and that Euridice is the twilight. As sun, Orpheus descended into an abyss of

---

* Edgar de Bruyne, *The Esthetics of the Middle Ages* (Ungar, 1969), p. 195.

darkness in the hope of overtaking his wife; in the morning, on turning round to look at her, he lost her again. *Meridian*, therefore, is the cocksure song sung by Orpheus at midday when his powers are at their zenith, the time, however, when he is farthest away from Euridice, the divine mystery, 'the image of love'.

The piece is scored for mezzo-sprano, horn and cello, two choirs of sopranos, two choirs of instruments (cors anglais doubling oboes and bass clarinets doubling soprano clarinets) and a choir of punctuating instruments: harps, piano and percussion. Once again there are three time dimensions. There is the time of the mezzo singing the Logue and the second Wyatt poem, time moving towards a conclusion: 'Now is this song both sung and past: My lute be still, for I have done'. Then there is the time of the horn and cello which perpetually evoke time past, for not only is their material cyclic, at one juncture they quote a substantial section of the horn and cello duet in *Tragoedia*. (It is not without relevance that at the first performance, *Tragoedia* was given in the first part of the programme, so that a deliberate effect of *déja vu* was created.)

Horn and cello symbolize a pair of lovers struggling to accommodate each other. Throughout the piece they unfold a duet broken only when the two instrumental choirs change to high instruments and they are silenced by a shrieking chorale. It is immediately after this that the mezzo speaks (rather than sings) the line: 'The song is lie or nonsense.'

Until that climax the instrumental choirs have created mobiles or the blurred textures discussed earlier. In other words, they give the impression of being temporally autonomous and far distant. This impression of landscape is enhanced by the vocal choirs with their echoes, moans and strange resonances; once again it is a surreal landscape, a landscape in which the various objects change perspective as mysteriously as in a dream. Time present, the third temporal dimension, has been evoked.

*Nenia, Dinah and Nick's Love Song* and *Meridian* are instances of a type of progressive evolution—characteristic of Birtwistle. In his next work, *The Fields of Sorrow* (39), he takes the progression a step further. Three layers are involved. He says:

The top layer is something that has come to full fruition in a previous piece and which is already in decline in the next piece. The second layer is something that has been thrown up in the previous piece, comes to fruition and into full bloom in the next piece. And the third layer is something that is like a seed and is in the process of germinating to appear in a later piece.

Then as an afterthought he adds: 'But there are many more layers than this, of course.'*

*The Fields of Sorrow* has a text by Ausonius which Helen Waddell included in her *Medieval Latin Lyrics*.† Its source is Virgil's description in *The Aeneid* of lovers wandering through the forest of Avernus in Hades: 'They wander in deep woods, in mournful light, amid long reeds and drowsy headed poppies...' The scoring is not dissimilar to that of *Meridian* except that now Birtwistle distributes the performers spatially so that distance is actual as well as implied. At the back of the platform are two solo sopranos wordlessly calling to each other from the two corners. In front of them a four-part choir rings out the text like a haphazardly tolled bell in the distance. Then come two pianos and a vibraphone sounding even more bell-like. At the front are three-part choirs of flutes, cors anglais, bassoons and bass clarinets. Plumb in the centre of them sits the soloist, the inevitable horn.

The first of Birtwistle's layers (the element that came to fruition in a previous piece but is now on the wane) is *Meridian*'s song and its mirror, the duet. These are placed at the centre of the three-part structure, but their relationship has changed. Song and duet are now one and the same; the horn plays a long song-like line partnered by the vibraphone in organum and rhythmic unison. As they wander through Avernus, the lovers have found perfect accord

Nevertheless, their duet is not the predominant element in the

* Michael Nyman, sleevenote to Decca HEAD 7.
† Helen Waddell, *Medieval Latin Lyrics* (Constable, 1929).

piece; the element in full fruition is that which colours and fills out this strange landscape, the echoing sopranos and the mobiles created by the choirs of instruments. These have now become mobiles within mobiles. In the first section, the leading players are given sets of short motifs to play in any order they like. In the next, while the horn and vibraphone unfold their duet, the four choirs join to form a homogeneous unit; but in the last section they split up so that here no less than nine mobiles are in motion at the same time. Against this, the sopranos continue to call, the bells to clang.

These bell-like sounds, specifically those from the two pianos, constitute the third of Birtwistle's layers, the element that will germinate to appear in *The Triumph of Time* (43). In this work, just when the ear longs for clarity after so many blurred textures, those bells appear like a shaft of light. Indeed, coming about two-thirds of the way through at the point of the golden mean, they constitute the focus of the piece. But they are not the only quotation Birtwistle uses in the work. Earlier the duet for horn and vibraphone appears in an amended form, then following that he quotes the whole of *Chorale from a Toy-Shop* (19), the short piece written five years earlier to celebrate Stravinsky's 85th birthday, a chorale for clock-work musicians playing just off key, just out of time. Once again, all three quotations are intended to give the impression of *déja vu*.

*The Triumph of Time* takes its title from the engraving by Pieter Brueghel the Elder depicting Time at the head of a procession with Death on a skinny nag and Fame on a resplendent elephant. Birtwistle came across it after he had planned the piece, but it easily fitted his scheme. In a note he says that musically the listener should imagine

> in the foreground, the overall image of the procession: a freeze-frame, only a sample of an event already in motion; parts of the procession must already have gone by, others are surely to come; a procession made up of a (necessarily) linked chain of material objects which have no necessary connexion with each other... in the background, recurrent procedures that are continuously there if only

seasonally—the maypole, a weather vane, the tides... the position of the spectator identical with the composer's during the process of composition...

Once the ethos of the piece had crystallized in his mind, the process of composition was fairly rapid. Finding the appropriate character, however, took about a year. His first effort looks like a cross between *An Imaginary Landscape* and *Grimethorpe Aria*. The opening consisted of a long floating aria for soprano saxophone accompanied by choirs of wind and percussion. As it approached the first climax a trumpet took over. This was interesting in itself, but could hardly be extended much further, nor would it fulfil the opportunity such an important commission from the Royal Philharmonic Orchestra offered. Instead of a continuous aria, then, he proposed 'a piece of music as the sum of musical objects, unrelated to each other, apart from one's decision to juxtapose them in space and time'.

Juxtaposing unrelated objects had been on the periphery of Birtwistle's thought ever since *Entr'actes and Sappho Fragments* and explains his choice of heterogeneous quotations. Jean Piaget, the Swiss psychologist noted for his work on the development of the cognitive functions in children, has pointed out that we group things together in two ways only. On the one hand, we place things together because they share certain properties or qualities, on the other because they share the same space or time. The first are logical groupings, independent of space or time; the second he calls infra-logical groupings, groupings independent of necessary connections. Birtwistle, in opposition to serialists, who practise a very logical system, leans toward the less abstract, more concrete infra-logical camp, and *The Triumph of Time* was intended as an affirmation of this.

Yet Birtwistle has never been happy with the work, even though many proclaim it a masterpiece. He feels it fails to affirm the infra-logical grouping and that the continuity is too smooth, too logical: 'It's just the piece they expected an avant-garde composer to write.' But despite his reservations it is superby written for its medium. The symphony orchestra was developed for the sake of spatial depth as well as for colour and power, and a processional is ideal for it. The techniques of suggesting distance by means of distortion, blurring and additional resonance are exploited to the full, and even greater emphasis is laid on differences between rates of change—what has been only implicit in the previous processionals now becomes explicit.

The piece is a huge *Adagio* of Mahlerian proportions, though as precursor the work which immediately springs to mind is the relatively short Funeral March from Webern's Op. 6. Most of the material changes constantly even though degrees of change vary. But two events stand out by virtue of their consistency. One represents time triumphant, the other time transcended. The first is a phrase of three notes played by an amplified soprano saxophone—a strange, unnerving sound repeated seven times without any alteration whatsoever. But like the bass clarinets in *Nenia* or the circling mobiles in *Meridian*, no sooner has it become predictable than it explodes into an ear-piercing chorale screamed out by all the high woodwind and the soprano saxophone at maximum amplification. Time the destroyer is revealed in all his terrible ruthlessness.

Time, however, fails to destroy the second event, a beautifully constructed tune for cor anglais, which on its three appearances, even though its context changes, is altered only slightly. On its first appearance its context is A, on its second E, while at the very end it is C. All these are satisfactory, but only the last feels inevitable. A closer inspection will reveal that it owes its inviolability to its tightness of construction. A bilateral pattern of graced notes is locked into a bilateral pattern of plain notes to create an inner structure of the highest tensile strength.

What distinguishes *The Triumph of Time* from the other processionals discussed is that the timelessness of this tune seems the *raison d'etre* of the piece. What lingers in the mind is time transcended rather than time triumphant. Birtwistle prides himself on his codas and in this one he has achieved almost the perfect casual exit. It departs, but is still there. In the remaining two processionals, *An Imaginary Landscape* and *Grimethorpe Aria*, his exploration of heterogeneous time within the extremes of destructive change and timelessness is approached from slightly different angles, but the codas of both provide the clue: in *An*

*Imaginary Landscape* it is a sombre chorale, in *Grimethorpe Aria* a poignant duet for two euphoniums, the distillation of the piece.

*An Imaginary Landscape* (38) was prior to *The Triumph of Time* and is the first of Birtwistle's pieces identified as a processional. He said:

> The musical procedure has an analogy with the way one experiences, visually, physically, a natural (or man-made) landscape. One starts, stops, moves around, looks at the overall view, fixes one's attention on a particular feature, or on a detail of that feature, or on a fragment of that detail, or on the texture of that fragment.

The scoring is for brass, percussion and double-basses distributed into choirs which partially re-form about halfway through. It was composed when he and Zinovieff were working on *Chronometer* (41), to date his one and only purely tape piece. Following John Cage, whose various Imaginary Landscapes all involve electronic processes of one kind or another, he fed information into Zinovieff's computer in the hope that this electronic process would give him some interesting proportions for the piece; but the results disappointed him and he amended them.

What is unusual about the work is that no soloists are involved; there are only choruses, groups of instruments. Indeed, the influence of Stockhausen's *Gruppen*, the work which revolutionized the use of space in music, is manifest. Stockhausen's description of his piece could also be used for *An Imaginary Landscape*. He talks about how the various groups separate or get closer and closer to each other, how one may receive another into itself, how they coalesce. 'Then all three orchestras become one—playing in the same tempo, the same harmony, the same hues.'* This is almost an exact account of how Birtwistle's groups gradually coalesce to play, as softly as possible, the deeply impressive closing chorale which, incidentally, he wrote in memory of his mother.

* Karl Wörner, *Stockhausen: Life and Works* (Faber and Faber, 1973), p. 38.

Such finales, however, are rare in Birtwistle; his attempts to freeze a moment of time tend to be confined to arias rather than chorales. In baroque opera, where they originated, arias were retrospective to action. All baroque scenes consisted of a recitative (action) and an aria (passion). In effect, arias stopped the flow of action, they froze a moment of time.

As with his other processionals, *Grimethorpe Aria* (45), has a three-dimensional temporal framework, but here they are much more evenly balanced. Time reversed is effected by the usual procedure of cyclically returning to previous material, time forwards by pressing to a climax, while timelessness is suggested by a continuous aria divided between horn and flugel horn.

It is a strange work to present to a northern brass band, whose repertoire, until the advent of its conductor, Elgar Howarth, used to consist of livelier, 'more ear-tickling fare'. Grimethorpe is a colliery village near Barnsley in Yorkshire, virtually at the heart of the great industrial belt which stretches across the black millstone grit of the central Pennines. If Birtwistle had a landscape in mind then it must be this, for the piece is as sombre as the Pennines themselves. He heads the score with a line from Blake's *Jerusalem*, not the well-known hymn, but the prophetic poem which also proclaims a new Jerusalem 'among these dark Satanic mills': 'Let the indefinite be explored, and let every man be judged by his own works.'

The exploration of the indefinite constitutes the essence of the piece. At the beginning the whole band quietly searches for a rhythm and a pitch. Then from the midst of its gropings, the flugel horn finds a tune. Against it are pitted jagged punctuating chords, apocalyptic fanfares and a chorale which eventually explodes in the now familiar manner.

But the tune blossoms into an aria and persists, continuing almost as if the surrounding vagaries and eruptions had not occurred. At the end the two euphoniums, in what must be one of the loveliest passages in all Birtwistle, summarize the aria in 'an elegiac cantilena', as Elgar Howarth describes it.

# 6: GEOMETRIA

BETWEEN *The Triumph of Time* and *Grimethorpe Aria* Birtwistle composed a short piece for Matrix which he subtitled *Eight Arias of Remembrance* (44). Based upon a short story of Alain Robbe-Grillet called *La Plage*, it is probably the closest he has ever come to the experimental music of such American composers as LaMonte Young or Morton Feldman in that it consists of only minimal change and little in the way of forward motion or climax.

The appeal of Robbe-Grillet's story is that it presents in literary form his central organizing principle: start with an absolutely regular and uniform pattern of the simplest, most predictable kind, then superimpose upon it a pattern which is its extreme opposite—something capricious and unpredictable. In the story are three absolutely regular patterns—the footsteps of three children walking undeviatingly along a beach on a fine, cloudless day in summer; the regular lap of a wave on the shore; and the regular progress of a flock of sea-birds moving parallel to the children. The fourth pattern, the chimes of a far-off bell, appears to be irregular and therefore unpredictable, for it is this which rouses the children's interest. The action of the story, the element that gives it shape, is their response to the bell: 'There's the bell.' 'It's the first bell.' 'Maybe it wasn't the first if we didn't hear the other, before . . . ' 'We'd have heard it the same.' 'We weren't so close before.' 'We're still a long way off.' 'There's the bell.' These seven sentences, intoned between the eight arias, which are not vocal but instrumental, constitute the text of Birtwistle's piece. Only once does the singer join the instruments, during the seventh aria, the *peripeteia* of the piece, when she is asked to wander freely through the notes played by the clarinets, as if singing to herself.

Once again, the temporal framework of the piece is three-dimensional, but now the emphasis has shifted more decisively than ever towards subjective time, neatly emphasized by the singing of the soprano to herself. Lacking a climax, other than when the singer joins the instruments, the sense of forward movement, though fundamental to time, is well-nigh absent; only minimal goal-orientation is suggested. Nor is long-term memory called into play; there are no quotations to provoke *déja vu*. The pace being slow, the impression is of time arrested.

Birtwistle and Robbe-Grillet share a view of time that owes much to the philosoper Henri Bergson. Bergson distinguishes two kinds of time. On the one hand there is clock time: a series of discrete, homogeneous points moving in a single direction, objective, intellectual time; time on a spatial model—Birtwistle's pulses, the regular lapping of the wave or flight of the birds in *La Plage*. On the other hand there is pure time: a continuous, heterogeneous flow in which past, present, and future are fused into what Bergson calls duration—subjective, intuitive time. In Bertrand Russell's* view,

> Bergson's theory of duration is bound up with his theory of memory. According to this theory, things remembered survive in memory, and thus interpenetrate present things: past and present are not mutually external, but are mingled in the unity of consciousness.

Bergson's own words make the relevance of the theory to *La Plage* even clearer:

* Bertrand Russell, *A History of Western Philosophy* (George Allen and Unwin, 1940), p. 834.

There are no two identical moments in the life of the same conscious being. Take the simplest sensation, suppose it constant, absorb in it the entire personality: the consciousness which will accompany this sensation cannot remain identical with itself for two consecutive moments, because the second moment always contains, over and above the first, the memory that the first has bequeathed to it. A consciousness which could experience two identical moments would be a consciousness without memory.*

The action of *La Plage*, the process which has a beginning, middle and end as opposed to the perpetually recurring lap of the wave and flight of the birds, is the comment of the children. In terms of information theory, which claims that the only unpredictable events are informative, the children are responding to the only information in the environment: the bell. In terms of Bergson's theory, their comments demonstrate the subjectivity of their response, each child interpreting the present in terms of its memory of its own past, its own perspective. But neither Robbe-Grillet nor Birtwistle are prepared to isolate subjective or pure time; both seek to place it within a context of clock time. In Birtwistle's case, this has been the position ever since *Ring a Dumb Carillon*. Here, in place of Robbe-Grillet's waves and birds, objective time is conveyed by the eight discrete, homogeneous and regular arias.

Objective time, being an absolutely regular and uniform pattern, corresponds to the first stage of Birtwistle's central organizing principle. But this principle applies to all aspects of a Birtwistle score: absolutely regular and uniform patterns, therefore, are the basis of the twelve-note *color*, where the intervals become progressively wider, and the eight-note *talea* where, in like manner, the durations become progressively longer.

Since Birtwistle demands more irregularity than the medieval practice would produce, two additional operations are

* J.J.C. Smart (ed.), *Problems of Space and Time* (Collier Macmillan, 1964), p. 140.

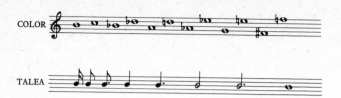

introduced. The first is logical: *talea* and the first eight notes of the *color* are placed in a matrix, so that certain pitches and certain durations occur more frequently than others. The second, however, is totally illogical. Underneath each note he writes a random number: whether generated by a computer or picked out of a hat is of no account, all that matters is that each is unpredictable.

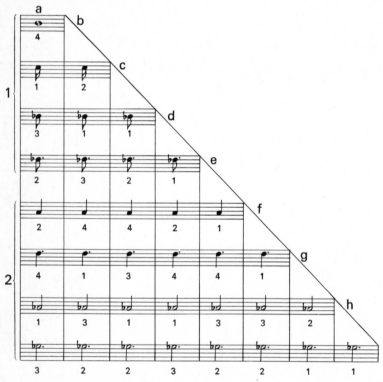

*The Music Theatre Ensemble performing* Down by the Greenwood Side *at the Brighton Festival in May 1969*

*Harrison Birtwistle during rehearsals with the Ballet Rambert in 1977*

ELECTRA    ELECTRA

ERA...    ...MNESTRA

(Malcolm Crowthers)

*Harrison Birtwistle in August 1981 during rehearsals at the National Theatre for Peter Hall's production of* The Oresteia

(Zoe Dominic)

*Original production of* Punch and Judy *at the Aldeburgh Festival in June 1968.
Scene from 'the Nightmare' where Judy is a fortune-teller and Pretty Poll a witch*

*Punch grieves over his murder of Choregos. Opera Factory production of* Punch
and Judy *at London's Action Space, January 1982*

(Christopher Lienhard)

*Harrison Birtwistle in 1983*

To obtain his aria he reads down each column in turn taking cognizance of the horizontal division and placing the notes in the order indicated by the numbers. The result has a certain waywardness about it, but the harmony is nicely centred on the polarities of A flat and E flat, while the durations become much more stable nearer the end. The pitch is transposed an octave, and those notes with a cross attached are either deliberate improvements or permitted mistakes!

Out of this simple line, Birtwistle creates a texture with three strands. The first is the aria itself. This he gives to the right hand of the piano. The second is the distancing effect created by the three clarinets which echo the piano and play out of tune so as to blur the pitch. The third is the bell, a single muffled toll rung in the left hand of the piano.

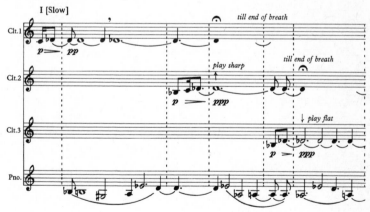

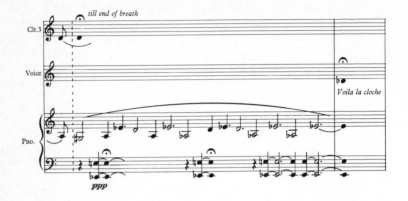

For the remaining arias *color* and *talea* are rotated, the tune is alternated between piano and clarinets, while the bell continues to be heard from different perspectives simultaneously or in sequence. The only new element is the increasing participation of the singer, so that by the seventh, like Mrs Green in *Down by the Greenwood Side*, she has entered 'the area of the others'.

Birtwistle's bias towards subjective time, particularly the time of those like Mrs Green and Orpheus who tend to brood, received additional stimulus when he came across Dürer's engraving *Melencolia I* as he was writing a piece to commemorate Tony Wright, the delightful melancholic who had done so much to promote his music on behalf of his publisher, Universal Edition. Dürer's engraving shows Melancholia as Geometria (symbol of the geometrical operations which lie behind art, craft, and many branches of natural philosophy) sitting alone deep in thought with the tools of her trade lying scattered around her. As Erwin Panofsky says in his book on Dürer:

His Melancholia is neither a miser nor a mental case, but a thinking being in perplexity. She does not hold on to an object which does not exist, but to a problem which cannot be solved.*

Borrowing Dürer's title, Birtwistle composed a piece for clarinet, harp, and two string orchestras which he dubbed his Tallis Fantasia. In itself it breaks no new ground, but it admirably focuses the issue of objective and subjective time as well as that of melancholy, the mood which seems to colour most, if not all, the works associated with Orpheus.

While he was composing the piece, Birtwistle read avidly not only Panofsky, but also the concluding essay in Günter Grass's *From the Diary of a Snail*. This is called 'On Stasis in Progress, Variations on Albrecht Dürer's Engraving Melencolia I'. Grass says that as he went round Germany campaigning on behalf of Willy Brandt,

> My creeping sole travelled the pathways of a society on whose fringes groups were beginning to take desperately extreme attitudes of resignation or euphoria. Daily flights into utopia found their counterpart in relapses into melancholic withdrawal.†

The burden of his argument is that stasis and progress, melancholy and utopia are heads and tails of the same coin.

> From time immemorial, the dead weight of things as they are has been played off against progress as the possibility of change. For wherever progress is frustrated by premature aims or utopian flights from reality, wherever its advances are so slight as to be ludicrous, the conservative who 'knew it all along' triumphs. His melancholy gestures signify that nothing can be changed, that all human effort is in vain, that an imponderable fate rules: human existence as doom.

* Erwin Panofsky, *The Life and Art of Albrecht Dürer* (Princeton University Press, 1971), p. 163.
† Günter Grass, From the Diary of a Snail (Penguin, 1976), p. 252.

Only order, a universally respected system, offers security.*

Grass concludes, only those who are melancholics,

> who know and respect stasis in progress, who have once and more than once given up, who have sat on an empty snail shell and experienced the dark side of utopia, can evaluate progress.†

Birtwistle would underline two points in particular: first, the complementary relationship of stasis and progress; second, the notion that for a melancholic 'only order, a universally respected system, offers security'. The Apollonian ring to this clearly relates it to Orpheus as well as to Birtwistle himself. Indeed, in his view, he and Orpheus are quintessential melancholics, simply because both of them are geometricians, both consider music 'a dance of numbers'. They are melancholic, according to the scholastic philosopher Henry of Ghent, because although good mathematicians, they are 'very bad metaphysicians'.‡ This was the point Erigena made about Orpheus quoted in connection with *Meridian*. To use Henry's words, Orpheus, and perhaps even Birtwistle too, are people 'in whom the imaginative power predominates over the cognitive one'. They

> will accept a demonstration only to that extent as their imagination can keep step with it... Their intellect cannot transcend the limits of imagination... and can only get hold of space or of that which has a location and position in space... whatever they think is a quantity, or is located in quantity, as is the case with the point. Therefore such men are melancholy, and become excellent mathematicians but very bad metaphysicians, for they cannot extend their

---

* Ibid., p. 257.
† Ibid., p. 271.
‡ This and the following three quotations are from Panofsky, p. 170.

thought beyond location and space which are the foundations of mathematics.

Concluding that Dürer's *Melencolia* is one of those who 'cannot extend their thought beyond the limits of space' Panofsky says in terms which apply perfectly to Orpheus: 'Hers is the inertia of a being which renounces what it could reach because it cannot reach for what it longs.'

At the end of this chapter we shall illustrate the extent of Birtwistle's fascination with 'the dance of numbers' when we examine a few bars of... *agm* ...; but at this juncture some general remarks about his use of geometries may be useful. He employs all three, Euclidean, projective, and topological, but unlike the serialists who tend to concentrate on simple Euclidean transformations such as transposition and inversion, he veers towards the more sophisticated projective and topological varieties. Projective geometry is concerned with properties which remain invariant when a figure casts a shadow on to a plane, as when a *talea* is projected on to a *color* in isorhythm. Topological geometry is concerned with properties unaffected by continuous distortion such as when a piece of elastic is twisted and stretched. When Birtwistle twists and stretches his basic cell in the manner discussed when dealing with *Cantata*, he retains the identity of the cell, so the operation can be deemed topological.

These two examples are but the tip of the iceberg. Birtwistle claims that he does not compose by intuition but by method. Indeed, he mistrusts intuition, believing that it produces only clichés; it regurgitates what has been supplied to it by nature or nurture; it can never create anything new. The only way the iron grip of necessity can be broken is to establish a situation which will automatically produce an accident. It could be a disaster, but equally, it could be a miracle.

As an example of an artist who produces miracles, Birtwistle cites Paul Klee. We have mentioned that Klee is a constant source of ideas, but none is so potent as Klee's unique combination of rigour and fantasy. Birtwistle is intrigued by the chart after chart of numbers Klee produced when preparing a picture; by the patterns, the tables, the diagrams he made. Many are reproduced in Klee's notebooks* where the editor places the working drawings and the finished picture side by side, so that, says Birtwistle, 'the transformation from the mechanical to the magical is there in front of you'.

His fascination was bound to lead to a homage to Klee. He combined it with a *bonne bouche* for the tenth anniversary of the London Sinfonietta, a piece ironically called *Carmen Arcadiae Mechanicae Perpetuum* (53) after Klee's *The Twittering Machine* (1922). Instead of four mechanical birds, Birtwistle's piece has six, 'juxtaposed many times without any form of transition'. Each obeys its own set of rules, but dynamics and register are independent. These have time-scales that are not coincidental with the mechanisms and so they have a life of their own. In other words, they are the jokers in the pack, the cause of disruptions, but also the source of magic.

To produce the artificial effect, Birtwistle tips the balance of his central organizing principle in favour of its first element: the predictable. By limiting the capricious element to dynamics and register he creates something bizarre, simply because dynamics and register are usually considered subservient to pitch and rhythm. When given their autonomy, the impression is unnatural.

Birtwistle creates this and all his other effects by self-consciously manipulating his central organizing principle, his system. The last time he composed something intuitively, from the top of his head, was in 1957. But he is not alone in his denigration of intuition, of 'self'. It is also the view of those who maintain that meaning can only be explained in terms of conventional systems, the view of structuralists such as Lévi-Strauss. Jonathan Culler says:

> once the conscious subject is deprived of its role as source of meaning, once meaning is explained in terms of conventional systems which may escape the grasp of the conscious subject, the self can no longer be identified with

* Paul Klee, *Notebooks*, ed. Jürg Spiller (Lund Humphries, 1961).

consciousness. It is 'dissolved' as its functions are taken up by a variety of interpersonal systems that operate through it. The human sciences, which begin by making man an object of knowledge, find, as their work advances, that 'man' disappears under structural analysis. 'The goal of the human sciences', writes Lévi-Strauss, 'is not to constitute man but to dissolve him.' (*La Pensée Sauvage*, p. 326). Michel Foucault argues in *Les Mots et les Choses*, 'that man is only a recent invention, a figure not yet two centuries old, a simple fold in our knowledge, and he will disappear as soon as that knowledge has found a new form'* (p. 15).

In other words, the self is not a centre nor a source but a construct, it has been put together by systems of convention, be they language, social codes, musical systems or whatever. To quote Heidegger, 'Language speaks. Man speaks only in so far as he artfully "complies" with language.'† Birtwistle's pre-occupation with self, although it reveals his introspection, merely reflects his passionate interest in systems of convention, his absorption in how things are constructed. He makes use of Jung's theories about the self, not because he is a devotee of analytic psychology, but because Jung has invented a rich allegorical language and deals with the relationship between the two basic conventional systems within the psyche so graphically.

Absolutely fundamental to Birtwistle, then, is the conviction that he is an inventor, someone who constructs. He might well agree with Michel Foucault's contention that in time man could disappear. What survives is not man but the systems man invents. The tighter, the more rigorous the system, the more likely is it to endure. In recent years archaeology has been favourite reading. He notes that those artefacts which were constructed systematically may have decayed, but their precepts enable them to be reconstructed. Their systems have transcended time.

---

* Jonathan Culler, *Structuralist Poetics* (Routledge and Kegan Paul, 1975), p. 28.
† Ibid., p. 29.

Nowhere has this been so vividly apparent than in the poetry of Sappho. In 1978, when he was searching for a text suitable for a major work commissioned by the Ensemble Inter-Contemporain for the John Alldis Choir and the Ensemble, his friend Tony Harrison suggested he use a set of Sappho poems known as the 'Crocodilopolis Cries'. These are fragments discovered in Fayum, the ancient Crocodilopolis. Seemingly most of Sappho's poetry found its way from Lesbos to Egypt where it was copied on to papyrus rolls. Later many of these rolls were torn into strips for the wrappings of mummies. At Crocodilopolis strips of papyrus with fragments of poems still on them were found stuffed into the jaws of mummified crocodiles. All that remains of the poems are an odd word here or there, part of a line or perhaps just a syllable. And yet it is possible to reconstruct not only individual lines but whole poems simply because so much is known about the metric systems Sappho used. With such patterns as the Sapphic stanza in front of them, scholars can fit the fragments into position, what is missing being deduced.

In the event, Birtwistle only used the fragments themselves, occasionally throwing in an English translation as a guide. He called the piece . . . *agm* . . . partly because *agma* means fragment, partly because the syllable *agm* occurs so often, and partly because 'agm' is an abbreviation of Agamemnon and Birtwistle was fascinated by the similarity between Sappho's metric grid and Clytemnestra's hunting-net which ultimately trapped Agamemnon. The work is scored for sixteen solo voices (SATB), a group of eleven high instruments, a group of nine low instruments, and six punctuating instruments. Birtwistle may be setting fragments, but . . . *agm* . . . is the least fragmentary piece he has ever composed. Its character is monumental, its texture absolutely cohesive.

It is also rigorously systematic and offers an excellent illustration of the dance of numbers. In particular, it shows how he 'tempers' his lines, and aspect of his work not yet considered. For the purpose of exegesis a phrase of fifteen notes about a quarter of the way in has been selected.

Basically it is a monody in E minor: high instruments playing it in one rhythm, low instruments in another, while the sopranos and altos, supported by certain percussion instruments, sustain a drone on F, the flat supertonic of E. To construct his monody, Birtwistle take the scale of E minor (E F sharp G A B C sharp D sharp) plus its flat supertonic (F) and flat sub-mediant (C) and arranges the notes into three symmetrically related five-note scales.

His next step is to give these scales shape. This he does automatically by numbers. Taking the numbers given beneath the scales above, he arranges the first group of five in the order 3 2 5 4 1. Then for the other two groups he repeats this ordering but varies it by advancing 5 two places and 41 one place. Only the advance of 41 is indicated; from it the advance of 5 should be self-evident.

Before discussing the rhythm, here is the phrase as it appears in the sketches before octave doublings, expression marks or dynamics have been added. Technically the two strands constitute two-part heterophony. Missing is the drone for voices and percussion. The asterisk indicates an alteration. The note should be C not A.

The rhythm is also determined by number. The lower line leads and dictates the pattern. It consists of five three-note phrases involving six durations ( ♪ ♩ ♩ ♩. 𝅝 ), the phrases arranged in two groups, two plus three. The numerical unit being the quaver, or eighth-note, this is the pattern of durations:

| GROUP 1 | | | | | | GROUP 2 | | | | | | |
|---|---|---|---|---|---|---|---|---|---|---|---|---|
| 1 | 6 | 1 | 3 | 1 | 3 | 8 | 6 | 2 | 1 | 8 | 6 | 4+2(6) | 8 |
| (8) | | | (7) | | | (16) | | | (15) | | | (14) | |

In each group one unit is subtracted from each successive phrase. In the first group the second phrase is the inverse of the first in terms of relative lengths. In the second group 86 regresses one place so that the pattern is similar to that governing pitch.

The upper line, on the other hand, does not seem to be determined by number. It can only be considered in relation to the lower line. The combined rhythm of the two lines develops a pattern moving from ♪♫♩ ♪♫♩ ♫♩ ♫♩ ... to the very regular and stable ... ♩ ♩ ♫♩ ♩. This is clearly not a mechanical operation, nor is the application of expression marks or dynamics. But octave doublings, or rather the way octave doublings are bent, are certainly controlled by number.

Octave doublings are one of the many ways in which a line can be thickened. At one extreme of this process lies heterophony, at the other the mere application of vibrato. Organum, whether it be at the octave, fifth or fourth, would occupy a middle position. Birtwistle, however, insists that the doublings or organum should have more information than they had in medieval practice, so he bends them with the use of adjacencies. These he places in four divisions. Here are the four divisions surrounding E.

Both the upper and lower lines of his monody are to be three octaves deep. To decide which octave should have which division, he devises a table not six but seven octaves deep. He starts with the highest octave for which he selects a four-figure pattern (indicating the four divisions) related to the five-figure pattern he selected for his monody 3 2 (5) 4 1. This is the complete table.

*Monody Notes*

| Octave | 1 | 2 | 3 | 4 | 5 | 6 | 7 | 8 | 9 | 10 | 11 | 12 | 13 | 14 | 15 |
|---|---|---|---|---|---|---|---|---|---|---|---|---|---|---|---|
| 7 | 3 | 2 | 4 | 1· | 3 | 2 | 4 | 1· | 3 | 2 | 4 | 1· | 3 | 2 | 4 |
| 6 | 1 | 3 | 1 | 4· | 1 | 3 | 1 | 4· | 2 | 4 | 3 | 2· | 4 | 1 | 3 |
| 5 | 4 | 1 | 3 | 2· | 2 | 2 | 4 | 2· | 4 | 1 | 2 | 4· | 1 | 3 | 1 |
| 4 | 2 | 4 | 2 | 3· | 4 | 1 | 3 | 2· | 1 | 3 | 1 | 3· | 2 | 4 | 2 |
| 3 | 4 | 2 | 3· | 1 | 4 | 2 | 3· | 1 | 4 | 2 | 3· | 1 | 4 | 2 | 3 |
| 2 | 3 | 1 | 4· | 2 | 3 | 4 | 2· | 4 | 1 | 3 | 1· | 4 | 1 | 3 | 1 |
| 1 | 1 | 3 | 1· | 4 | 2 | 1 | 4· | 3 | 2 | 4 | 2· | 2 | 4 | 1 | 4 |

In columns beneath the top line are logical permutations of the basic figure (3 2 4 1). The figures in the lowest three lines are either a simple permutation of those in the upper four lines (i.e. the 3 2 4 1 of line 7 becomes 4 2 3 1 in line 3) or retrogrades of them (line 2 being the retrograde of line 6, line 1 of line 5). In the event, Birtwistle eliminates line 1, this octave being too high for the instruments at his disposal.

Having decided where to place the divisions, Birtwistle clearly needs a pruning mechanism. There are far too many notes. He therefore devises another table to limit the divisions. At the moment, each note in both the upper and lower lines of the monody has nine possible positions. This table reduces that number to 5, 6 or 7.

| Monody Notes | 1 | 2 | 3 | 4 | 5 | 6 | 7 | 8 | 9 | 10 | 11 | 12 | 13 | 14 | 15 |
|---|---|---|---|---|---|---|---|---|---|---|---|---|---|---|---|
| Upper line | 7 | 5 | 6 | 5 | 7 | 6 | 7 | 6 | 5 | 6 | 7 | 5 | 6 | 5 | 7 |
| Lower line | 7 | 5 | 6 | 5 | 7 | 6 | 5 | 6 | 7 | 6 | 7 | 5 | 6 | 5 | 7 |

The next step is the last. To decide which of the nine positions to retain, which to discard, Birtwistle now uses purely random numbers. For the sake of brevity we shall take only the first 7 notes of the upper line. The figures crossed out are those above the figure given in the table above. Once again there is an alteration (the number of notes required for the first note of the monody).

| Monody Note | 1 | 2 | 3 | 4 | 5 | 6 | 7 |
|---|---|---|---|---|---|---|---|
| Random Number | ~~7~~ 4 ~~9~~ | 2 1 7 | 7 5 4 | 1 ~~6~~ 2 | 2 ~~8~~ ~~9~~ | 2 1 5 | ~~8~~ 7 3 |
| | 5 6 2 | 3 ~~8~~ 4 | ~~8~~ 6 ~~9~~ | ~~8~~ 3 7 | 4 5 3 | 4 3 6 | 5 6 4 |
| | 3 1 ~~8~~ | ~~9~~ 5 ~~6~~ | 1 3 2 | 4 5 ~~9~~ | 7 1 6 | ~~9~~ ~~8~~ ~~7~~ | 2 1 ~~9~~ |
| Amount required | 7(6) | 5 | 6 | 5 | 7 | 6 | 7 |

This table should then be applied to the divisions selected earlier. For instance, for the first note of the monody in the upper of the two lines divisions 1, 4 and 2 were selected. Therefore D sharp is the central note. Cross out those notes as indicated above.

| | | | |
|---|---|---|---|
| Division 1 | ~~D~~ | D sharp | E |
| Division 4 | D | D sharp | F |
| Division 2 | C sharp | D sharp | ~~E~~ |

Here are those first seven notes of the upper line as they appear in the score. Even more alterations (or mistakes) have occurred. The system is such that mistakes must be tolerated.

The question is: could this system survive the ravages of time, or are the events too idiosyncratic to be reconstructed? Would *Geometria* endure?

# 7: PULSE

ALTHOUGH ITS FUNCTION varies from work to work, pulse has been a feature of Birtwistle's music ever since *Ring a Dumb Carillon*, but in four pieces of the Orpheus period he has given it particular emphasis: *Chronometer*, *Silbury Air*, *Pulse Field* and *Pulse Sampler*.

Originally, Birtwistle began to pit 'regularly recurring, precisely equivalent stimuli'* against his additive rhythms because it enabled him to time his fluid progressions against an objective standard. An additional bonus was its compliance with his central organizing principle. The first movement of *Verses* for clarinet and piano illustrated this admirably. Later it became evident that capricious patterns need not be devised additively, but could be produced when pulses moving at different velocities were superimposed upon each other and essential accidents occurred. This is what *Chronometer*, his tape piece, explores.

But before discussing it, mention must be made of his use of pulse in the music he composed for the 1981 production of *The Oresteia* at the National Theatre. Despite the complexity of the tables and charts we produced to illustrate his preoccupation with systems, with the dance of numbers, Birtwistle's material is

---

* Grosvenor Cooper and Leonard B. Meyer, *The Rhythmic Structure of Music* (University of Chicago Press, Phoenix edition, 1963), p. 3.

essentially simple, and over the years the tendency has been to reduce it still further. If his basic resources are a line built out of the simplest of melodic and rhythmic cells and filled out merely by duplication at the fourth, fifth or octave, there are times when even these are too complex for him and he turns to the most elementary material of all: 'pulse and drone and simple harmonies'. This desire for sparsity also extends to his use of music in the theatre, which must be necessary, must grow naturally out of a dramatic situation and not be cosmetic. In an interview he gave to Andrew Clements before the production of *The Oresteia*, he said, 'I usually find myself recommending to producers *not* to include music in their new productions.'

In the event, his music for *The Oresteia* was the production's saving grace. Not only did his use of pulse compensate for the lack of rhythmic variety in the translation, it provided the necessary beat for the chorus, paced the action, timed the climaxes and, above all, gave the affair a powerful sense of something primeval lying beneath the surface of events, something only a phenomenon as elemental as pulse could suggest.

Birtwistle strives to attain this elemental, mysterious quality in all his pulse pieces, even those, such as *Chronometer* (41), which start from the most prosaic of ideas, the sounds made by clocks: ticks, chimes, the whirr of springs and cogs. No other piece so successfully converts objective time, the time of clocks, into subjective time. On Birtwistle's behalf, Peter Zinovieff made some hundred recordings of clocks of all descriptions, analysed them by computer and, on the composer's instructions, regenerated the chosen montage on to eight-track tape. Basically there are four types of material. The first consists of ticks laid against each other like strands of counterpoint, and underpinned by the ostinato of Big Ben. But no clockwork mechanism, no tick, is absolutely regular (at least to the perceiver) and when Birtwistle exaggerates the irregularities they become more and more like hearbeats. After a while, the throb of Big Ben turns into that other definition of pulse: the rhythmical contraction and expansion of an artery. The effect is like the throb in the ear heard in bed at night.

In addition to ticks there are textures which seem to derive from cogs and springs—'a number of very dense, short, fast-moving structures with complex dynamics', Zinovieff calls them. They are one of two devices injected into the piece to disturb what well might become too soothing. The other is even more of an irritant, 'three two-minute interludes of very fast complex sounds where every change is preceded by a short pure signal'. The effect is like a tape played too fast, or, more pertinently, like accelerated motion in the cinema. While these interludes last, everything else freezes. Birtwistle used 'frozen frames' in *Punch and Judy*, and in *The Mask of Orpheus* he elevates them to a principle. In the cinema they are used to create the effect of time suspended. *Elvira Madigan*, for instance, ends with a 'frozen frame' of the young heroine reaching out to catch a butterfly in a cornfield. It coincides with the sound of the shot which kills her. Birtwistle uses 'frozen frames' for various purposes, but in *Chronometer* the purpose is to heighten the surreal, the dream-like quality of the piece.

The fourth element, the element which draws the structure together and closes it, also serves this purpose. It is the chime of one of the oldest clocks in the country, that of Wells Cathedral. For most of the piece eerie transformations of it have punctuated the texture at strategic moments, but at the end its full chime is given. Objective time, clock time, has once again intruded itself upon us.

Bells frequently appear in Birtwistle. We first encountered them when discussing his arrangement of Machaut's *Hoquetus David*. They were then mentioned in connection with *Verses* for clarinet and piano, *Dinah and Nick's Love Song*, *The Fields of Sorrow*, *The Triumph of Time* and *La Plage*. What is interesting about them is that, like the ticks of clocks, they ought to be absolutely regular yet rarely are. Sometimes the mechanism or the bell-ringer may be at fault, but more often than not the unevenness is caused by clang-tones and beats within the bells themselves. In extreme cases of unevenness they appear to be set in motion by the wind or currents of air like mobiles. This is the effect Birtwistle usually seeks to achieve. Some bells, however, are designed to be tolled by nature—the warning bells on buoys out at sea, for instance:

> And under the oppression of the silent fog
> The tolling bell
> Measures time not our time, rung by the unhurried
> Ground swell, a time
> Older than the time of chronometers...*

Birtwistle made devastating use of such a bell in *Prologue* (37), his setting of the Watchman's speech from the *Agamemnon* for tenor and seven instruments. At the beginning of the play the Watchman is on look-out for the beacon which will indicate victory in Troy, but since only sound or movement can be indicated in music, Birtwistle transfers the signal to a notional bell clanging ominously out at sea. When the singer reaches the words 'A man's will nurses hope' it peals out, not in joy, but terrifying menace. Once again the impression of an elemental rhythm has been conveyed, the rhythm of something 'sullen, untamed and intractable'.†

On the whole the use of bells occurs in pieces not overtly concerned with pulse. In *Silbury Air* (50), where pulse predominates, the only bell-like sounds are the four peremptory harp chords which end the work (they also end *Melencolia I*). In his programme note, Birtwistle tells us that although the work is named after Silbury Hill, the mysterious prehistoric mound near Avebury in Wiltshire, it should be considered 'a compound artificial landscape or "imaginary landscape", to use Paul Klee's title', a landscape 'presenting musical ideas through the juxtaposition and repetition of "static blocks" or . . . objects'. He fails to point out that the score is prefaced with what he calls a 'pulse labyrinth', four zigzagging tables of metric divisions and metronome marks, which are clearly much more relevant to the organization of the piece than anything he mentions in his note. This is the fourth table:

---

* T. S. Eliot, 'The Dry Salvages' from *Four Quartets* (Faber and Faber, 1944), p. 26.
† Ibid. p. 25.

107

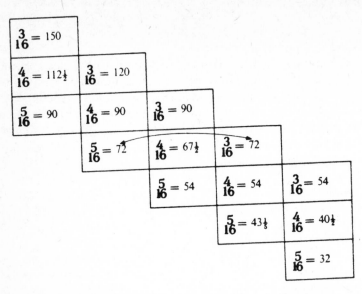

The pattern is fairly self-evident: the vertical columns co-ordinate the units (semi-quavers or sixteenth-notes) arranging them into groups (i.e., bars) of three, four or five; the horizontal lines coordinate the metronome marks—any figure divided by a higher figure to left or right of it yields $\cdot 9375$ $\left(\frac{15}{16}\right)$.

Essentially Birtwistle has provided for himself a means of changing gear either by preserving the unit or the metronome mark. For example, the first three metric changes in the piece involve preserving the unit $\left(\frac{4}{16} = 90, \frac{5}{16} = 72, \frac{4}{16} = 90, \frac{3}{16} = 120\right)$; the next involves preserving the metronome mark $\left(\frac{3}{16} = 120, \frac{4}{16} = 120\right)$. This means that although the ticking of pulse is constant in this section, sometimes the grouping may change, sometimes the velocity. As the work proceeds, change occurs quite rapidly and various groupings and velocities are superimposed upon each other. Essentially the labyrinth is a map charting possible routes but offering no solution. Each change must be made on whim. In other words, the labyrinth represents yet another variant of the central organizing principle: first establish a logical foundation then act on it illogically. Three times Birtwistle sets out to find his way out of the labyrinth only to find himself back at his starting point. When he does discover the exit, indicated by the four harp chords cutting abruptly across the start of a new cycle, it is purely by chance.

But Birtwistle is not content to restrict the analogy to the prosaic level; he also pursues its allegorical ramifications—that is, he uses the labyrinth as a symbol. This applies particularly to certain aspects of texture and structure. There are times when the texture becomes so convoluted that one has the sense of being lost inside some elaborate maze. There are other times when the structure suggests the spiral shape of a labyrinth. Even the pulse labyrinth at the beginning of the score, with its zigzagging pattern, resembles a spiral. According to Jill Purce, the spiral is not only the natural form of growth (this alone would recommend it to Birtwistle), it also has personal and cosmic significance.

> The spiral tendency within each one of us is the longing for and growth towards wholeness. Every whole is cyclic, and has a beginning, a middle and an end. It starts from a point, expands and differentiates, contracts and disappears into the point once more... If life is a path 'through' time, and therefore a continuum, we may also imagine it as a line; and further, since it returns and yet flows on, it is a spiral. Only if it were possible to come back to the *same point in time* could it be a circle. Any circular movement carried into the fourth dimension (of space-time) becomes a spiral; which is why apparently cyclic processes in time never repeat themselves. Even the earth's orbit round the sun is a spiral in time, and every year is different from the last.*

Given Birtwistle's preoccupation with cyclic forms which return but are always different, the concept of a spiral or a labyrinth was bound to be significant. Indeed, the route through Hades which Orpheus follows is traditionally an inward-

---

*Jill Purce, *The Mystic Spiral* (Thames and Hudson, 1974), p. 13.

winding spiral or labyrinth, as is the route for all who wish to transcend time, the spiral being a symbol for the progress of the soul towards eternity.

In the light of Jill Purce's remarks, the large sections of Birtwistle's works, variously called cycles or strophes, are more aptly gyrations of a spiral. In *Silbury Air*, where on completion of each cycle the music returns to the same pitch (E), the same bar length ($\frac{4}{16}$), the same instruments (string quintet) and the same dynamic (*pppp*), but not to the same velocity, the concept seems entirely justified.

In this instance the spiral is contracting and thus dissolving. But Birtwistle never confines the structure to one dimension. As always there is an independent element which straddles the whole piece and is responsible for closure in that it describes a single rather than a recurring arc. The clue to this is embedded in the title: it is not Silbury Hill, but *Silbury Air*. In other words, the element is melody which emerges out of the pulsations, takes shape in the woodwind during the first gyration and flowers in the second. But in contrast to the ever-insistent pulses with which it is contrasted, there is something elusive about it. Even when it culminates in a chorale-like texture near the end of the second gyration, it seems more like an airy mobile than a purposeful tune. Nevertheless, it carries the weight of the piece and when it sinks to its lowest point closure is merely a formality. Hence the use of chords which have already brought another piece to an end.

Birtwistle's next work, *Pulse Field* (51) or, to give it its original title, *Frames, Pulses and Interruptions*, was his one and only excursion into ballet. Ballet Rambert had asked him to collaborate with the Dutch choreographer, Jaap Flier, and although the work has never been revived since the original performances in 1977, it excited a great deal of interest at the time because the two men were clearly at loggerheads. Jaap Flier told the *Time Out* reporter:

> In the early days Harrison and I became quite aggressive towards each other. He felt that he must discover how dancers think before he could start writing the score. As he

is very mathematical and methodical he kept asking questions. But dancers are very intuitive, and think with their bodies, so they felt his questions were very stupid. They resented being asked to do simple movements over and over so he could analyse the mechanics. I would wait for him to compose some music, and he would wait for me to give him some steps.

At that time Birtwistle was working with Tony Harrison on a threatre piece called *Bow Down* (52), a piece for four musicians and five actors based on various versions of the Ballad of the Two Sisters. Since joining the National Theatre, he had become convinced that music in the theatre was more effective when it was not incidental but integral. The model he kept before him was Japanese theatre where actors, dancers and musicians are interchangeable. In *Bow Down* the musicians form part of the chorus, while the actors dance, sing and play instruments. The nine sit in a semi-circle within which the drama is performed. This sharing of roles inevitably imposes simplicity on the musical means, but as we have noted, this spareness is what Birtwistle desires. Everything stems from a simple pulse and three basic intervals.

'The very economy of the music', reported William Mann in *The Times*, '—drumbeats, gently hummed chords, sparce plaints for two oboes—served to heighten the presentation's hieratic slowness to an almost Kabuki-like intensity.'

This was the situation Birtwistle hoped to achieve with *Pulse Field*. 'I had an idea about relating music with dance—not in relation to structure but to content and form', he said.*

> I'm interested in working in a theatrical situation which is like a workshop—working on the floor of a theatre as opposed to working at home... I've tried to set up an acoustical situation which is to do with pulse, with the

---

* *Dance and Dancers*, July 1977, pp. 17-18.

basic elements of music—pulse and drone and simple harmonies.

When he and Flier eventually began to see eye to eye, Flier made some simple 'boxes' or 'frames' of dance, which they placed in a certain sequence, then at the end stretched them all out, elongated them in time. 'I think we got down to a sort of lowest common denominator of music and movement', continued Birtwistle.

The musicians are on stage: four percussion-players, one at each corner; two double-basses, amplified, one at either side; and three trombones across the back. This meant a cueing system between players, and between players and dancers...

The 'frames' or 'boxes' are recurring events not unlike the gyrations of *Silbury Air* but much shorter. From time to time all the dancers, except one, 'freeze' on a musical interruption, and stay that way until the music starts again. The person outside this 'game' is a single female dancer who creates a continuous line throughout the piece, often providing comic commentary to the slow, measured patterns of the others.

Birtwistle's score, like the score he wrote for Les Percussions de Strasbourg a year earlier—*For O, for O, the Hobbyhorse is Forgot* (49)—is merely an outline to be filled by the players in rehearsal or performance—a synopsis. The main directions: 'faster than' and 'slower than' indicate the relative nature of the situation.

*Pulse Sampler* (59) for oboe and claves, his most recent pulse piece, formalizes these directions. Throughout, the oboist, who is always one tempo behind the claves player, is precisely 'faster than' or 'slower than'. If *Bow Down* and *Pulse Field* reflect the hieratic spareness of Japanese music, especially Gagaku, *Pulse Sampler* mirrors the *jeu de rapport* of Indian music. This is not only evident from its formal attributes, the oboist playing the *raga*, the claves player the *tala*, but also from the wit of the piece, the 'understanding' between the players, even their hierarchical status, for the claves player must sit at the oboist's feet like an

112

acolyte in attendance. What is not Indian is the asperity and dryness of the sound. Indeed, for most of the time the oboist must be as desiccated and brittle as the claves. Although a relatively modest piece, *Pulse Sampler* summarizes much of what has gone before. Its central feature is a pulse mobile given to the claves player: four rhythmic cells which can be varied at will provided that the order is preserved ( ♩♩ ¸♩¸♩ ¦♩ ¦♩ ♩ ). A cell may be repeated any number of times or missed out. The exception is the first cell which must always begin each mobile and end each period or section. Within each period the mobile, or parts of it, will appear several times, the length being determined by the material given to the oboe. But each time the period changes the tempo changes. In *Silbury Air* there were nineteen different tempi, here there are only six, but their relations are the same. In every instance the claves player samples the tempi in advance of the oboist, and Birtwistle warns that 'there is not to be any synchronization of tempi between the two players; rather a mechanical independence is to be achieved'.

Structurally the work contains twenty-eight periods divided into two groups of fourteen, each a vortex in that each contains four twists of a spiral whirling towards a climax. At the climax of the second, oboe and claves momentarily coincide with each other. Thereafter the mobile is reinstated in its original form, and the work ends with a peremptory stroke on a wood block.

*Pulse Sampler* may summarize many of the tendencies developed in previous works, but it cannot begin to précis the use of pulse in the composer's *magnum opus*. That needs a chapter to itself.

# 8: THE MASK OF ORPHEUS

ON THE SURFACE, BIRTWISTLE seems to be paradoxical; nevertheless his thought is essentially cohesive. He is a hedgehog, not a fox; to paraphrase Sir Isaiah Berlin: he relates everything to a single, central vision, one system less or more coherent or articulate, in terms of which he understands, thinks and feels—a single, universal, organizing principle in terms of which alone all that he is and says has significance.

This single central vision of his has two facets: one relates to the act of doing, the other to the act of perceiving—one is a rational process, the other intuitive. For Birtwistle doing is composing, a rational process made 'informative' by the controlled application of chance. Perceiving, however, involves absorbing a variety of perspectives simultaneously, and this can only be done intuitively.

That music in its highest manifestation is a rational phenomenon was first put forward by the Roman philosopher Boethius whose text about Orpheus Birtwistle set in *On The Sheer Threshold of the Night* (57). At the root of Boethius' ideas is the Pythagorean concept that *music is number made audible*. It demonstrates in sound the pure world of mathematics and derives its beauty from that world. According to Dorothy Koenigsberger, Boethius's view can be expressed analogically.

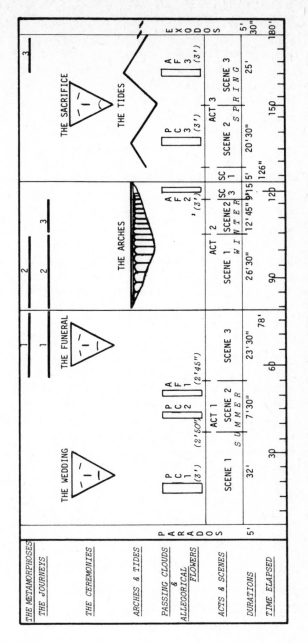

*Peter Zinovieff's chart of the structure of* The Mask of Orpheus.

Men can easily recognize a triangle when they see one, but, at the same time, they cannot know the properties of a triangle *a priori*. They must learn arithmetic and geometry to understand these properties. In the same way men have to study the mathematical sciences to know what they hear; for human beings appreciate music by use of reason, not by the ear alone. Although consonance and dissonance are initially perceived, they are not understood until men comprehend them through the science of number.*

Boethius distinguished three kinds of music, *musica mundana* (the harmony of the spheres), *musica humana* (the seasons and the elements), *musica instrumentalis* (voices and instruments); and three kinds of musicians.

One class has to do with instruments, another invents songs, a third judges the work of instruments and the song. But that class which is dedicated to instruments and there consumes its entire efforts... are separated from the intellect of musical science, since they are servants... nor do they bear anything of reason, being wholly destitute of speculation. The second class having to do with music is that of the poets, which is borne to song not so much by speculation and reason as by a certain natural instinct. Thus this class also is to be separated from music. The third is that which assumes the skill of judging, so that it weighs rhythms and melodies and the whole of song. And seeing that the whole is founded in reason and speculation, this class is rightly reckoned as musical, and that man as a musician who possesses the faculty of judging, according to speculation of reason...†

In Boethius' opinion Orpheus lost Euridice because he was not a *musicus*, a theorist, but a mere *cantor*, a singer. *On the Sheer*

---

* Dorothy Koenigsberger, *Renaissance Man and Creative Thinking.* Harvester Press, 1979, p. 178.
† Oliver Strunk, *Source Readings in Music History* (Norton, 1950), p. 86.

*Threshold of the Night* is part of the poem which ends Book III of *The Consolation of Philosophy*. Throughout this work, written when Boethius was imprisoned and under sentence of death for alleged conspiracy against the Emperor, he compares the stability of reason with the fickleness of fortune, and Orpheus is introduced to point the moral of his case. Had Orpheus been a *musicus* he would have kept his eyes on the light of reason, the sun shining in front of him. Instead he cast his lot with fortune, obeyed the intuitive law of love, turned, and lost. 'Ye who read, look up: the gods in daylight dwell. All that you hold of loveliness sinks from you, looking down at Hell.'

Birtwistle's setting is a madrigal for four solo voices (soprano, counter-tenor, tenor, and bass) and twelve-part mixed chorus. In it the choice between reason and intuition has psychological as well as philosophical significance. The singers are arranged in an arc at the centre of which are the counter-tenor and tenor, who sing the role of Orpheus in rhythmic unison. Usually such duplications represent the voice of God, as in Britten's canticle *Abraham and Isaac* or Stravinsky's *The Flood*, but here the purpose is to indicate the two sides of Orpheus' nature, the two options open to him. That his anima is sung by a counter-tenor and not by an alto is a clue to his psychological plight. To the left of this pair are ranged the men, to the right the women. The men press the claims of the ego (reason), the women the claims of the anima (intuition); throughout the piece the two pull against each other. But when the decision is made they merge: 'Yet is not love his greater law? And who for lovers shall decree?' In turning away from reason, however, Orpheus has lost all that is reliable: 'On the sheer threshold of the night Orpheus saw Euridice, looked, and destroyed her.'

In the opera there is no distinction between *cantor* and *musicus*. On the contrary, as the disciple of Apollo, Orpheus is the very embodiment of reason. He has already made the choice, already cut himself off from the natural, sensuous side of life, before the action begins. But before taking this further we must place Birtwistle's position vis-à-vis the rational act of composing and the intuitive act of perceiving in context. It is not as contradictory as it may seem. One refers to the way in which he finds his material and proliferates it, the other to how he structures it. Both are aspects of a predominantly right-hemispheric mentality.

The study of how the two hemispheres of the brain function is still in its infancy, but it would appear that quite different modes of consciousness are involved. Robert Ornstein says:

> Although each hemisphere shares the potential for many functions, and both sides participate in most activities, in the normal person the two hemispheres tend to specialize. The left hemisphere (connected to the right side of the body) is predominantly involved with analytic, logical thinking, especially in verbal and mathematical functions. Its mode of operation is primarily linear. This hemisphere seems to process information sequentially. This mode of operation of necessity must underlie logical thought, since logic depends on sequence and order. Language and mathematics, both left-hemisphere activities, also depend predominantly on linear time. If the left hemisphere is specialized for analysis, the right hemisphere ( ... connected to the left side of the body) seems specialized for holistic mentation. Its language ability is quite limited. This hemisphere is primarily responsible for our orientation in space, artistic endeavour, crafts, body image, recognition of faces. It processes information more diffusely than does the left hemisphere, and its responsibilities demand a ready integration of many inputs at once. If the left hemisphere can be termed predominantly analytic and sequential in its operation, then the right hemisphere is more holistic and relational, and more simultaneous in its mode of operation.[*]

All that has been said about Birtwistle's preoccupation with spatial objects and landscapes, his bias towards infra-logical as opposed to logical groupings, his preference for non-linear

[*] Robert Ornstein, *The Psychology of the Consciousness* (W. H. Freeman, 1972), p. 51.

118

progressions, his cyclic forms, his use of simultaneities, indicate how right-hemispheric his thinking is. So too does his rational method of composition, for in reality it only concerns the manipulation of numerical patterns; no true mathematical, analytic or logical thinking is actually involved. Although the acts of composing and perceiving belong to the same mode of consciousness, Birtwistle can quite legitimately place the claims of reason and intuition he extracts from them into dramatic conflict because one is active or creative, the other passive or receptive. The psychological dilemma facing Orpheus, as symbolized in his relation with his wife, represents the condition of all those who place creativity above receptiveness, action above passion. In this respect *The Mask of Orpheus* resembles *Punch and Judy*.

Birtwistle's appositional way of thinking has inevitably drawn him to a form of theatre where holistic presentation takes precedence over linear plot. This happens even when the philosophy is alien to his own. An example is the Theatre of the Absurd (the theatre of Adamov, Beckett, Genet and Ionesco); at no time has he ever subscribed to the central tenet that life is meaningless and hence essentially absurd, nevertheless Martin Esslin's résumé accords with everything he himself aims to do in the theatre:

> Like ancient Greek tragedy and the medieval mystery plays and baroque allegories, the Theatre of the Absurd is intent on making its audience aware of man's precarious and mysterious position in the universe... While former attempts at confronting man with the ultimate realities of his condition projected a coherent and generally recognized version of the truth, the Theatre of the Absurd merely communicates one poet's most intimate and personal intuition of the human situation, his own *sense of being*, his individual vision of the world. This is the *subject-matter* of the Theatre of the Absurd, and it determines its *form*, which must, of necessity, represent a convention of the stage basically different from the 'realistic' theatre of our time... It is a theatre of situation as against a theatre of

119

events in sequence, and therefore it uses a language based on patterns of concrete images rather than argument and discursive speech... While the play with a linear plot describes a development in time, in a dramatic form that presents a concretized poetic image the play's extension in time is purely incidental. Expressing an *intuition in depth*, it should ideally be apprehended *in a single moment*, and only because it is physically impossible to present so complex an image in an instant does it have to be spread over a period of time. The formal structure of such a play is, therefore, merely a device to express a complex total image by unfolding it in a sequence of interacting elements.*

This holds good for all Birtwistle's music, but it is particularly evident in *The Mask of Orpheus*. Some conception of its 'intuition in depth' may be gained by the devices for separation it requires. One is a movable stage capable of dividing an upper action from a lower one:

'All action for the outside world is shown on the upper stage and that of the underworld on the lower stage', Peter Zinovieff, the librettist, explains.

> The two types of action may take place at the same time. The diference in level of 'over' and 'under' is also the difference between life and death, between fact and fantasy and between Man (or Hero) and Myth.†

Another is a further division of the stage by means of two rivers, one horizontal, the other vertical. 'Almost continuously throughout the opera there are at least two simultaneous threads to the plot. These may be two simultaneous slightly different versions of the same thing or completely unrelated actions.' The upper and lower stages being limited to upper and lower divisions, the rivers provide lateral separation and can be

---

* Martin Esslin, *The Theatre of the Absurd* (Penguin, 1968), p. 392.
† Zinovieff has produced three editions of the libretto. This quotation comes from the first, but the second has also been drawn upon.

moved along their horizontal and vertical coordinates to provide greater flexibility.

Yet another division is supplied by a vehicle called The Golden Carriage of Mirrors which may be likened to the *Flugwerk* used by the three boys in *The Magic Flute*. This moves up and down as well as laterally and 'allows a journey to be made within it while protecting the passenger from the stage situation'. In Act II Orpheus descends to the underworld in it; as a consequence he can remain aloof from the terrifying visions surrounding him.

These are devices of spatial separation, but time is also divided: past, present and future are independent entities which need not follow in linear progression. This becomes prevalent in the last act, but 'words, action and music have echoes and pre-echoes throughout the work'. As might be expected in a Birtwistle piece, some events are returned to over and over again; but

> this is always accompanied by some distortion such as the event being from another character's viewpoint. For instance the death of Euridice is seen at least five times from different situations and each time represents a new judgement.

Another very discriminating feature is that at times words, action and music do not coordinate with each other, but behave quite independently.

The most startling device for achieving 'intuition in depth', however, comes from the duplication of roles. Each of the three main characters, Orpheus, Euridice and Aristaeus, has three forms. As human beings they are represented by masked singers, as heroic figures by masked mimes, as myths by very elaborate puppets with voices coming from amplified singers offstage. Orpheus is also shown as a destructible paper effigy, while Euridice's other forms include a doll, a small puppet and a huge immobile puppet. All forms can be on stage at the same time.

These and many other features undoubtedly stem from another form of contemporary theatre which is non-linear:

Antonin Artaud's Theatre of Cruelty. It is no coincidence that Birtwistle was embarking on *Punch and Judy* when the finest example of it in Britain was staged—Peter Brook's production of *The Marat/Sade*. Artaud considered that 'drama's job was to express things which could not be put into words', that it ought 'to liberate forces in [the] audience's subconscious... by giving direct expression to their dreams and obsessions...'*

'Practically speaking', said Artaud, 'we want to bring back the idea of total theatre, where theatre will recapture from cinema, music-hall, the circus and life itself, those things that always belonged to it.'† And he goes on to say:

> Every show will contain a physical and objective element, perceptible to all. Cries, groans, apparitions, surprises, theatricalities of all kinds, magic beauty of costumes taken from certain ritual models; resplendent lighting, incantational beauty of voices, the charms of harmony, rare notes of music, colours of objects, physical rhythm of movements whose crescendo and decrescendo will accord exactly with the pulsation of movements familiar to everyone, concrete appearances of new and surprising objects, masks, effigies yards high, sudden changes of light, the physical action of light which arouses sensations of heat and cold, etc.‡

Effusive though this description is, Birtwistle complies with all it suggests. But not even Artaud could have foreseen the lengths to which *The Mask of Orpheus* pushes the Theatre of Cruelty. Traditionally, opera libretti are modest affairs—that of *Parsifal* can be printed on less than thirty pages—but Zinovieff's is as diffuse as a film director's script. Indeed, it needs to be for film technique is precisely the means by which Birtwistle achieves his radical innovations and his documentation is necessarily

---

* John Russell Taylor, *The Penguin Dictionary of Theatre* (1970), p. 21.
† Antonin Artaud, *The Theatre and its Double* (Calder and Boyars, 1970), p. 66.
‡ Eric Bentley, *The Theory of the Modern Stage* (Penguin, 1976) p. 59, quoting Mary Caroline Richards' translation of *The Theatre and its Double*.

voluminous. He has always been interested in the cinema, its influence being particularly apparent in the techniques he uses to convey subjective time: 'the cinema can either imitate exactly the time of the physical world, or can modify it radically', say Ralph Stephenson and J. R. Debrix.*

> By modifying it, the cinema can, as Robbe-Grillet suggests, assemble on the screen, by various means, but principally by montage, something more like the time of our mental than our physical life—a mixture of future, past, and present, passing over some events in a flash, dwelling on others, returning to others. Something less continuous, less predictable, less inflexible than the time of the physical world.

We have already noted Birtwistle's use of frozen, slow and accelerated motion, but he is equally indebted to montage. In this respect he owes much to his mentors Satie and Stravinsky. Satie was the first composer to realize that montage, the editing and cutting of the film, should be applied to film music as well, while Stravinsky applied the principle to all his scores. Edward Cone called it stratification: 'the separation in musical space of ideas—or better, of musical areas—juxtaposed in time'.† A vivid example occurs at the end of *Orpheus* where a fugue is twice interrupted (Stravinsky said 'cut off with a pair of scissors') in order to insert two extraneous bars for harp.

In *The Mask of Orpheus* the most extensive use of montage occurs in the structures called the Arches and the Tides which dominate Acts II and III. These will be discussed later, but it also occurs in the Passing Clouds of Abandon and the Allegorical Flowers of Reason, six interludes of mime and electronic music which are cut into the action so as to surprise not only the audience but the principal singers, and perhaps even the conductor as well. While they last everything else is

---

* Ralph Stephenson and J. R. Debrix, *The Cinema as Art* (Penguin, 1976), p. 124.
† Benjamin B. Boretz and Edward T. Cone (eds.), *Perspectives on Schoenberg and Stravinsky* (Norton, 1972), p. 156.

frozen. Each is about three minutes long, utterly self-contained and played by a special group of actors at a pace so accelerated that 'they will always leave a leisurely pace behind them, even if the main action was fast, for nothing could be faster than the clouds'. The Passing Clouds of Abandon concern Dionysus, the god whom Orpheus opposes, and provide clues to the murders which take place: the Allegorical Flowers of Reason concern Apollo and comment on the love story.

All the Dionysian stories anticipate the tearing apart of Orpheus by the Maenads. The first concerns the death and resurrection of Dionysus himself; the second the mutilation of someone who opposed Dionysus; the third the mutilation of someone who opposes followers of Dionysus. These are clearly violent; the Apollonion stories, however, are lyrical. All come from Ovid and are three of the many stories told by Orpheus on top of his hill as examples of the transformations of lovers such as Hyacinth and Dryope into flowers.

Birtwistle regards all six clouds as essential to the opera on three grounds: they are so clearly unrelated to the main action 'that the notion of other simpler but simultaneous action must become easier to accept'; they allow 'a more satisfactory distribution of the points of main tension'; they epitomize the emergence of myths, for *The Mask of Orpheus* 'is about the birth and death of music, words, intelligence and religion, the clouds emphasizing the mythological transitions shown in the story as a whole'.

The gist of the story is more or less the same as outlined at the beginning of Chapter five. One major difference is that the descent into Hades is portrayed as a dream. Zinovieff says in the libretto:

> This is not a trivial change. The plot is concerned over and over again with the state of mind of Orpheus and, to a lesser degree, of Euridice. There could be no clutter with actually portraying a myth. Myths are recounted not seen.

As a consequence the plot changes overtly into a

psychological allegory and consequently draws heavily on Jung. Indeed the description of Orpheus in the *dramatis personae* paraphrases Jung's very words: 'He is a passive character. He arouses violence ' or love in others. His emotions are mainly cerebral—that is not to say intellectual but of the mind'. In the opera Aristaeus is called the shadow (the unconscious 'natural' side of a human being), while Euridice is presumably his anima (the unconscious feminine side of a man).

According to Jung:

> the inferior half of the personality (the shadow) is for the greater part unconscious. It does not denote the whole of the unconscious, but only the personal segment of it. The anima, on the other hand, so far as she is distinguished from the shadow, personifies the collective unconscious.*

Thus we have returned to Birtwistle's central dramatic issue: the conflict between the ego and the collective unconscious. But since *Punch and Judy* a shift has taken place in the relationship, a shift we noted when discussing *Nomos* and *Linoi*. Whereas in *Punch and Judy* a capricious ego wilfully represses the collective unconscious within him then recovers it after a dream, in *The Mask or Orpheus* a passive, withdrawn ego unwittingly represses, or perhaps merely suppresses his collective unconscious. He, too, dreams, but to no avail, for in this case he fails to recover what is lost. At the end the compensatory forces in the psyche, symbolized by the Maenads, overwhelm and destroy him.

As in *Punch and Judy*, the time span covers the cycle of the year. Act I, which deals with the wedding of Orpheus and Euridice, her seduction by Aristaeus and her funeral, takes place in summer; Act II, the descent into Hades, takes place in winter; Act III, the sacrifice, in spring. Each act has three scenes subdivided into three sections, while framing the work is a Parados expressing the birth of intellect, 'the transition from sounds into music, from syllables into words, from inaction into

---

* C. G. Jung, *The Archetypes and the Collective Unconscious* (Routledge and Kegan Paul, 1959), p. 215.

action' and an Exodos in which Aristaeus placates the gods and has his bees restored to him.

Dominating the whole opera, however, is the cyclic transit of the sun. 'The sun represents Orphism, Apollo and Reason'. The Parados opens with the rising of the sun and apart from a period during Act II when Orpheus descends to the lowest depths of Hades it is present throughout. Nevertheless it changes constantly: 'it can change its size; change colour and brightness; become patterned like a target; move vertically and horizontally; have the shadow of a bird projected across it'. In the Exodos, when it represents the Orphic egg, it divides into three parts as if hatching. The significance of the Orphic egg occasionally mentioned in classical sources is historically an enigma, but both Jane Harrison* and W. K. C. Guthrie† agree that it probably represents the birth of Eros, the god of love, more specifically the god of desire, of sexual love. Thus at the very end, just as the Green Man occurs at the end of *Punch and Judy* and *Down by the Greenwood Side*, Birtwistle presents us with a symbol of fertility and renewal, a hint that the attribute Orpheus lacks has at last been awakened.

Since Birtwistle intended to include as many layers as possible, the inclusion of Orphism was inevitable. However, Orphism was a mystery religion and very little is known about it. All that can be said is that it preached 'a belief in the essential immortality and divinity of the human soul, and the necessity for constant ritual purity if that immortality were not to be forefeited'.‡ Zinovieff says that his text forms 'one long set of poems which are structured around a type of Orphic cosmogeny' but this cosmogeny has had to be invented for the purpose of the opera. So too has an Orphic language, an invention particularly appealing for Birtwistle since it reinforces the fact that the whole affair is an invention, that, like Stravinsky, he and Zinovieff have created an archaic world virtually from scratch. This invented language occurs in the

* Jane Harrison, *Prolegomena to the Study of Greek Religion* (Merlin Press, 1962).
† W. K. C. Guthrie, *Orpheus and Greek Religion* (Methuen, 1935).
‡ W. K. C. Guthrie, *The Greeks and Their Gods* (Methuen, 1968), p. 317.

song Orpheus sings as he watches his head drifting downstream on the river Hebrus uttering strange prophecies. The vocabulary consists of 151 words made from the phonemes of 'Orpheus' and 'Euridice'.

Birtwistle calls the song the Third Song of Magic. Like *Punch and Judy*, *The Mask of Orpheus* is a number opera, but now the numbers are ordered systematically. Altogether there are 123 arranged in 41 groups of 3, most of them being recitatives or arias. Of the arias, undoubtedly the most important are Orpheus' three Songs of Magic. As in all the groups, a trend is defined, a movement from one mood to another: 'Very virtuous' is the overall designation of them. 'Become simpler and purer. Use special alphabet (ultimately the invented language). First is fireworks. Second moving, the third distorted.'

These Songs of Magic occur within three very Orphic substructures: the Ceremonies (the Wedding and Funeral in Act I, the Sacrifice in Act III), the Arches of Act II and the Tides of Act III.

'The Ceremonies are secret ritualistic dances which, by repetition and exposition of a gross and inner detailed structure, gradually become revealed as parts of a sacrificial murder.' If the tenets of Orphism can be expressed only in general terms, the rituals of the faith are even more obscure. Jane Harrison believed they were strongly linked to Dionysian rites:

> The full significance, the higher spiritual developments of the religion of Dionysos are only understood through the doctrine of Orpheus, and the doctrine of Orpheus apart from the religion of Dionysos is a dead letter.*

She then quotes the philosopher Diodorus to support this: 'Orpheus, being a man gifted by nature and highly trained above all others, *made many modifications in the orgiastic rites*: hence they call the rites that took their rise from Dionysos, Orphic.' Following this, she says:

* *Op. cit.*, p. 454.

The great step that Orpheus took was that, while he kept the old Bacchic faith that man might become a god, he altered the conception of what a god was, and he sought to obtain that godhead by wholly different means. The grace he sought was not physical intoxication but spiritual ecstasy, the means he adopted not drunkenness but abstinence and rites of purification.

She then makes a list of possible ceremonies ranging from the Dionysian rite of tearing apart flesh and eating it raw, to what she believes was the final Orphic custom: the mimetic celebration of a sacred marriage which symbolized belief in spiritual union with the divine.

Thus, in proceeding from a wedding to an orgiastic sacrifice the opera reverses the historic process: 'The three ceremonies', says Zinovieff,

represent the backwards evolution in man's development. The sacrifice shows his most decadent and pleasure-seeking side—even to his own destruction. The wedding— the first ceremony—is the most advanced. Here man dominates nature and artificially introduces a structure that is intellectually or aesthetically pleasing. The funeral, half way to the sacrifice, shows man at his most animal-like. His grief refuses too much artificiality whether it is of the body (sacrifice) or of the mind (wedding).

This reversal of time, dramatically necessary because it gathers tension for the climactic sacrifice ('the wedding and funeral are, in fact, rehearsals for the final scene where Orpheus is torn apart, eaten and destroyed'), is in accordance with the practice Birtwistle follows in most if not all of his works: the balancing of forward with backward temporal movement (or the illusion of it). One practice, the most consistent, is perpetually to go over the same material again and again; another is to make the second half of a work the mirror image of the first, as in *Tragoedia*. This is yet another. But whatever the means, the purpose remains the same: to express a complex total image perceived as if it were a single, timeless moment.

Each of the ceremonies takes place within the following sequence: recitative, major aria, ceremony, silence, magic song and then dance, the climax of the proceedings. The celebrants are a caller, three priests and Orpheus puppet and Euridice either as singer or puppet. Since the ceremonies are secret and meant to be continuous, the audience only has glimpses of them. From time to time they are illuminated by very bright lights flashing on and off. At the core of each is a pattern of three exchanges, cryptic questions and answers between caller and priests and Orpheus, which 'set up a pattern for the dance'. This is the most cryptic event of all. It takes place around the imaginary limbs of a horizontal Tree of Life. Six dance figures are involved, but it is only when the positions of the dancers are 'freed' that Orpheus, as the sun, reveals the tree's true nature.

The ceremonies are esoteric, but the funeral at the end of Act I is undoubtedly the most complex, for here no less than three different events take place simultaneously: the funeral, the metamorphosis of Euridice from human being to huge immobile puppet, and the encounter between Orpheus and the Oracle of the Dead, the only character not yet mentioned. Orpheus promises her the secrets of his music in return for the secrets of the underworld, viz. always face the way of the sun, choose without choosing, never address anyone directly. However, he tricks her, for when she tries to sing all that comes out is a wretched screeching and croaking. According to Jung, the trickster is an archetype representing the mythical hero at a rudimentary stage of his development, 'a primitive "cosmic" being of *divine-animal* nature'.* Above all, as Punch had previously demonstrated, the trickster is a symbol of immaturity.

In the event, Orpheus does not require the secrets of the underworld for his journey takes place in dream. Act II is framed by a time shift showing a gigantic Euridice being clumsily killed by two monstrous snakes and the first death of

---

* C. G. Jung, *The Archetypes and the Collective Unconscious* (Routledge and Kegan Paul, 1959), p. 264.

Orpheus, one of the possible deaths offered by tradition, death by suicide. These are comparatively short; the bulk of the action concerns the journey on which he sings the seventeen verses of the huge second Song of Magic. In the course of this the other characters doubling as Hades, Persephone, Charon and Hecate interject with isolated words, screams, shouts, groans.

This song gives Birtwistle his one and only opportunity to involve his oldest structural manoeuvre—not the juxtaposition of contrasting blocks or numbers, but the continuous flow of isorhythmic cycles, each differentiated in mood and colour, the whole being controlled by an overall strategy which is itself cyclic. To make this dramatically viable 'an imaginary, visionary architectural structure' called the Arches is suggested, a structure the producer should regard as a model rather than a dictate. The drawings provided in the libretto show an aqueduct with seventeen arches traversing a valley, on one side of which lies the mountain of the living, on the other the mountain of the dead. At the bottom of the valley flows a river running from past to present; to complete this process the water in the aqueduct flows towards the future. Each arch represents a specific attribute of the world and the mood associated with it in Orpheus's mind—Countryside/Hesitancy, Crowds/Confidence; but the nearer they are to the mountain of the dead the narrower they become, the more restricted, the more terrifying—Buildings/Fear, Knives/Terror. It is this narrowing of the dimensions which governs the overall strategy of the song.

Each of its verses, each cycle, is in four parts: dream (aria), fantasy (recitative), nightmare (speech) then silence. Since Orpheus is moving consistently towards nightmare which will force him to wake up with a jolt, turn his face from the sun then lose the lingering trace of Euridice, so the proportions of each verse will alter to favour nightmare. To parallel the narrowing of each successive arch, Birtwistle shortens each verse by three seconds. The proportions of the first are: dream, 2 minutes 20 seconds, fantasy, 14 seconds, nightmare, 30 seconds; while those of the fifteenth, the verse in which Orpheus wakes up screaming 'a wild animal cry of terror' are: dream, 7 seconds, fantasy, 6 seconds, nightmare, 1 minute 53 seconds.

The last two arches constitute the last scene of the act, the period when the sleeper becomes aware of the dream's implications. The Golden Carriage of Mirrors which transported Orpheus through Hades has disappeared. Now in his mind's eye he sees a re-run of the events in shadow play. His puppet voice sings the last two verses of the Song of Magic offstage; the second cloud of Allegorical Flowers of Reason passes (the story of Apollo and Hyacinth); in despair Orpheus realizes the truth and hangs himself.

But this is only his first death; he must suffer three more. The second, his death by a thunderbolt thrown by Zeus for betraying the secrets of the gods, occurs near the beginning of Act III; his third at the hands of the Maenads takes up the bulk of that act, and involves the structure which the authors call the Tides; his last happens near the end. This is when the prophecies issuing from his skull on the island of Lesbos are finally silenced by the jealous Apollo.

If the Arches are artificial, the Tides are natural. They are the means by which Birtwistle can involve the second of his two structural manoeuvres, the juxtaposition of contrasting blocks, more autonomously than in the rest of the opera. They are also the means by which he can focus on his concept of time most succinctly, for they allow him to present past, present and future as if they were happening simultaneously. Once again, as in *La Plage*, he is concerned with events on a beach, and once again the structure is a model rather than a dictate.

We must imagine a beach with six objects on it washed by the ebb and flow of the tide. These objects are musical as well as physical: the two nearest the sea belong to the past, the three further up the beach to the present, while the highest belongs to the future. All are associated with death or decay and refer to a specific event. They are (1) a fossil shell (the death of Euridice; words and music very little changed); (2) an oar (the awakening of Orpheus from his nightmare; words and music from the last arches); (3) a fishing-net (Orpheus killed by Zeus); (4) a bird skull (Orpheus attacked and torn apart by the Maenads); (5) a footprint (Orpheus' head floating to the shore); and (6) a rockfall (Orpheus silenced by the jealous Apollo for daring to be god-like). The sequences 3 4 5, being events taking place in the present, form part of the third ceremony, the sacrifice.

The order in which these occur depends on the ebb and flow of the tide. On the rising tide each event lasts two minutes, on the ebbing tide two and a half minutes with an additional half-minute period for transition. There are two high tides, the second being the higher. The sequence is therefore: 3 4 (first rising tide) 4 3 2 1 (first falling tide) 1 2 3 4 5 6 (second rising tide) 6 5 4 (second falling tide). On each occasion the music and action are affected by how the event is triggered. Those on the first rising tide are considered 'from before' (that is, they are forecast and therefore distorted); those on the first falling tide 'from behind' (they face away and are thus partially obscured); those on the second rising tide 'actual' (they follow each other in chronological order and are consequently as factual—and horrific—as possible); while those on the second falling tide face 'towards silence' (their behaviour is erratic and always decaying).

Part two of this chapter illustrates how this unusual structure works, but first the important contribution of electronic music must be discussed. It is this, as much as anything, which conveys both the ambience of a beach and the ebb and flow of the tide.

Originally Birtwistle assumed that Zinovieff would realize the electronic music, but Zinovieff withdrew from this field in the mid-seventies and so Birtwistle sought the cooperation of IRCAM (L'institut de Recherche et de Coordination Acoustique/Musique) in Paris for assistance. Here the facilities are so sophisticated that what was originally intended to be fairly rudimentary has become almost as complex as the score.

The first two acts of the score, which were composed between autumn 1973 and spring 1975, bring to fruition the seeds planted in such now-familiar works as *Nenia*, *The Triumph of Time* and *Grimethorpe Aria*. There is an expansion of vocal techniques and the orchestral texture has become denser, a tendency Birtwistle develops to an even greater degree later. Indeed, so dense is the texture on occasion that a second conductor is required to assist in the direction. It is the second conductor who controls the orchestral continuum, an ever-present pattern so prominent in the second act.

Between the composition of the first two acts the third lay a gap of some six years during which were written *Melencolia I*, *Silbury Air* and ... *agm* ... . Inevitably a shift in style can be discerned. Not as great perhaps as the difference between the second and third acts of Wagner's *Siegfried* which were also separated by a number of years, but nevertheless the difference is there. The textures are even denser, the mood more hieratic. Birtwistle says that returning to the opera after so many years was 'murder'. It took him six weeks before he could pick up the threads again. 'It was the worst period of my life. I nearly went out of my mind, particularly since I hadn't quite finished the second act. It was very, very hard.'

He first contacted IRCAM in 1981. Amongst his collaborators were Jean-Baptist Barrière and Xavier Rodet of the *Chant* team. *Chant* is a project primarily concerned with analysing and synthesizing the human voice by means of computer. Birtwistle felt the sound of synthesized voices it produced was exactly what he wanted for the voice of Apollo. An example of the initial result of their collaboration may be found on the gramophone record issued by IRCAM (IRCAM 0001) where it has the title *Naissance du langage*. Later, these sounds became more structured when Barry Anderson became his principal collaborator. Between February of that year and August 1983, he and Barry Anderson, who is himself a composer, created about an hour's worth of music which colleagues at IRCAM consider some of the finest ever produced by the institute.

Three different types of material are involved. The first two, those of the Auras (atmospheric sounds to suggest summer in Act I, winter in Act II, tides and bees in Act III) and the six mime interludes (the Passing Clouds and the Allegorical Flowers) need two four-track reel-to-reel systems to reproduce them, while the third, which contains the voice of Apollo and requires to be cued with absolute precision, needs (ideally) a computer-based system. Although each system is quadraphonic the purpose is not to flood the auditorium but to extend the proscenium laterally and in depth.

Among the loudspeakers will be some needed to amplify

certain singers, both on and off stage, and certain members of the orchestra in the pit, particularly the three pedal harps which have to be set in relief in order to balance the modified or synthesized harp sounds on tape.

The simplest of the three types of material is that of the Auras. It consists of streams of atmospheric noise generated by the huge banks of oscillators (about 2,000) available at IRCAM. With these, evocations of the rustle of leaves, the howl of the wind, the swish of the sea, and the hum of bees were produced, all with rather sinister overtones. The most structured of them is that of the Tides. As well as evoking the ambience of the beach it indicates where the tide is at any one moment. The band width was narrowed so that statistically a specific pitch can be heard, the note E, the opera's principal pole of attraction. To each object on the beach Birtwistle ascribes a specific octave. To the fossil shell at the bottom of the beach he delegates the lowest E, to the rockfall at the top of the beach the highest. When the tide covers or uncovers an object the octave changes and a sense of ebb and flow is achieved.

The mime interludes, on the other hand, are complex. Each is an independent composition in its own right even though all share the same material and the same metric organization. The material stems from notes and chords of a harp analysed and resynthesized by computer to produce what Birtwistle calls 'a mad, mechanical percussion instrument'. Altogether, there are some 400 individual sounds. At one end of the spectrum are the sounds of what could be a bass drum; at the other those of an impossibly high piano, while lying between come marimbas, bongos, vibraphones or guitars.

According to Barry Anderson, the 'voicing' of the pieces was left to him, while Birtwistle concentrated on 'the critical thing', the rhythmic organization. He became fascinated by the ability of computers to divide a second into, say, 13 or 7 with absolute precision. As a result, he produced for the three violent Passing Clouds music Barry Anderson describes as 'diabolical, hair-raising'. The Allegorical Flowers mirror them in structure, but Apollonian lyricism and tenderness replace the Dionysian frenzy. This was achieved by careful selection of frequency areas rather than alteration to the material or metric organization.

Being derived from the notes of the harp, the basic material of the mime interludes consists of the same 'envelope': a fairly rapid onset transient, a decisive peak then a slow decay. On the Apollo tape these are combined with synthesized sounds of the human voice, sounds with the opposite tendency: a slow onset followed by a rapid decay after the peak. In musical terms the result is a long vocal upbeat, a downbeat in the form of a reinforced shout, then a reverberating afterbeat—the perfect envelope for the imperious voice of Apollo barking out some command aided and abetted by an emphatic twang of his lyre. The language he uses is Orphic, the gnomic language only a god may speak.

Altogether there are some 70 of these 'signals' from Apollo. They range from single gestures lasting a few seconds to miniature compositions of nearly a minute. Birtwistle scatters them throughout the opera in order to create the impression that Apollo controls everything, that he is like some heavy-handed father forever laying down the law.

The extent of Apollo's involvement grew out of the sessions at IRCAM: it was an afterthought. As a result Birtwistle intends to rewrite the opening Parados of the opera where Apollo gives birth to language and teaches Orpheus 'the magic of music and poetry'. But all in all this, and other slight changes which will have to be made, ought to clarify one of the opera's central issues, that whereas in other versions of the legend Apollo apotheosizes Orpheus, in this he condemns him. Here Orpheus commits the unforgivable sin of hubris. In singing the third Song of Magic in the forbidden tongue he indicates his aspiration to divinity. There is only one possible consequence: Apollo must destroy him.

To give an illustration of how these various elements are coordinated and organized in the opera, the opening of the second scene of Act III has been selected. This involves the first four sequences of the Tides: those of the first rising tide (the uncovering of the fishing-net and the bird skull) and those of the first falling tide (the covering of the bird skull and the fishing-net). After the first sequence the third ceremony, the sacrifice, begins.

This is how Peter Zinovieff summarizes Scene 1 of Act III:

> The act opens with a short scene of about 5 minutes. In this a substitute for the end of Act 2 is found in the rebirth of Orpheus into a gigantic red articulated puppet which grows through the elevated stage. This is the 3rd Time Shift.
>
> The first two Time Shifts showed the death of Euridice. This shows the evolution of Orpheus into a strong and magnificent mythological figure.
>
> A huge green sun shines. The sun slowly changes into a target against which much of the rest of the act is played. There are no words or vocal sounds in the first scene which is, therefore, an overture to the rest of the act.

## SEQUENCE 3   (Orpheus is killed by a thunderbolt)
Tide covers the fishing-net: events witnessed 'from before'.

ACTION: Orpheus and Aristaeus Puppets construct a huge destructible paper puppet of Orpheus. This is then destroyed by a thunderbolt. In Zinovieff's words, 'The puppets cross sides of the stage.'

SCENERY: On the right a mountainside; behind, the sun as a target starts dim, becomes bright and ends as at dusk; traversing the stage the horizontal and vertical rivers positioned so as to obscure the action.

WORDS AND MUSIC: Text and vocal line formal, but orchestral texture (which is part of a substructure) continuous and through-composed. It leads to the climax at the 3rd Terrible Death. In the pit a chorus of men's voices sustain chords using vowel sounds associated with the invented language.

(1) 1st Recitative of Teaching (Recitative of Thought)

136

Aristaeus Puppet (in *Sprechgesang*—clipped and staccato)

> *These are the branches!*
> *Dip the cut grass*
> *Into the clear Autumn streams.*
> *Carve the gold rocks*
> *Into the frozen masks.*
> *It is time:*
> *The animals are still.*

(2) 1st Aria of Prophecy (Aria of Achievement)
Orpheus Puppet (lyrically—with precise pitches)

> *On the hillside,*
> *His heart will blunten his white knife*
> *On the shadow of her flat memory.*
> *Birds lie locked to the hillside.*

(3) 1st Sentence of Religion (Sentence of Dogma)
Orpheus and Aristaeus Puppets in duet (hocketing)

> *I built this stone shelter,*
> *Over the dark cave.*
> *The soil is now ready for the new child.*

(4) 3rd Terrible Death (Death by Thunderbolt)
Orchestra (violently)
Exit Aristaeus Puppet

APOLLO TAPE: Word Command

RESPONSE II: Loud flourish then soft throbbing chord.
Pitch of Aura tape gradually moves up an octave.

# SEQUENCE 4 (3rd Ceremony: the sacrifice, 1st exchange)
Tide covers the bird skull: events witnessed 'from before'.

ACTION: Enter the Troupe of Ceremony and the Three Women
(the voices of Euridice Singer and Puppet come from off-stage).

137

Later Orpheus Singer appears at the side of the stage as an observer. Orpheus Puppet is approached and surrounded by the Troupe of Ceremony, attacked then destroyed. (This third ceremony is cyclic. Later Orpheus Puppet will be torn apart, eaten, have his bones scattered over the earth, and his head thrown in the river. The other three exchanges will start and end at different points in the cycle.)

SCENERY: The mountainside disappears; the sun becomes huge; the horizontal river is lowered, but the vertical river still partially obscures the action.

WORDS AND MUSIC: To a certain extent, these are independent of the action. They form a different cycle, a cycle with 11 sections: shout, question, extension of love duet, demand, invocation (complicated question), reply, statement, dance, silence, scream and song (trio). Whereas only part of the action cycle is given in an exchange, the whole of the words and music cycle always appears even though beginning and ending at different points. The orchestral texture is less through-composed, more overtly coordinated with the text and vocal lines.

(1) Shout: The Three Priests
> *Answer, answer, answer!*

2nd Dangerous Murmur (Murmur of Women)
12-part chorus (in pit)
> STAND, CLUTCH, PRESS, WAIT

(2) Question: The Three Priests
> *Where are the roots?*
> *Where the branches?*
> *Where is the tree?*

(3) 7th extension of 1st Love Duet: Euridice Singer and Puppet (off-stage), Orpheus Puppet.
> E.S. *I offered hand, asking, telling*
> E.P. *Orpheus, Orpheus*
> O.P. *I crowned songs, asking, telling*

138

(4) Demand: The Three Priests

> *Answer, answer, answer!*

(5) Invocation: 3rd Complicated Question (the Enigma)
The Caller (savagely)

> *Scream luckwards,*
> *Gold*
> *Fierce fire-time.*

(6) Reply: Orpheus Puppet (very simply)

> THIS TREE

(7) Statement: 3rd Look of Loneliness (Look of Love)
The Three Priests, the Caller and Chorus (in pit)

> *Here are the roots.*
> *Here are the branches.*
> *Here is the tree.*
> *This is the answer.*
> STAND, CLUTCH, PRESS, WAIT.

(8) Dance: 3rd Immortal Dance (Sacrificial Dance)

APOLLO TAPE

(9) Silence: Orpheus Singer from side of the stage, as if addressing the orchestra

> *Taste, Remember, Speak.*

(10) Scream: The Three Priests

> *Answer, Answer, Answer!*

(11) Song: 3rd Hidden Trio (Trio of Abandon)
The Three Women (gently)

> *White sorrow winds we slowly breathe.*

3rd ALLEGORICAL FLOWER OF REASON (The Lotus): Action and music freeze. A mime troupe enters and accompanied by electronic music mimes the following story (this is Zinovieff's version):

'Beautiful Dryope was feeding her infant at her breast by the edge of a pool. She picked some flowers and saw, to her horror, blood fall from them. She had not known that Lotus, a nymph, had changed herself into the flowers to escape from Priapus' lust. Dryope prayed to the water nymphs and tried to leave but she was slowly transformed into a lotus tree. Her husband and father protected the tree from animals and allowed her son to play under the shade of what had been his mother.'

(11)  Song (continued)

> *White sorrow winds we slowly breathe.*
> Chorus: STAND, CLUTCH, PRESS, WAIT.

   Aura tape fades

3rd SONG OF MAGIC The Song of the Tides, verse 4: Sung by Orpheus Singer from side of stage which is now in darkness. It covers the 'transition' period, the extra time required for the falling tide. Its music is the simplest in the opera: each short stanza is accompanied by a percussion continuum and punctuated gently by wind chords. Orpheus sings in the invented language. This is a translation!

1) *The object! What lies on the beach?*
   *A bird skull.*

2) *The strange object! What does the observer see?*
   *A young naked woman, moaning.*

3) *The fantasy! What the observer imagines.*
   *A sand clock, noting the months and years.*

4) *The first action! What the observer does to it.*
   *Hides it cunningly.*

5) *The second action! What does the tide do?*
   *Turns it over and over.*

140

6) *The symbol! What they remember.*
   *The first noticed dawn.*

7) *The pretence! What do they pretend?*
   *Fear and understand*

Aura tape recurs

APOLLO TAPE: Word Command.

RESPONSE II: (as before)

# SEQUENCE 4 (3rd Ceremony: 2nd exchange)
Tide uncovers the bird skull: events witnessed 'from behind', that is the singers and actors play to the back of the stage rather than to the audience.

ACTION: Starts at the point when Orpheus Puppet is attacked and ends when he is dismembered.

SCENERY: As before, but now both rivers are to the side so none of the action is obscured.

WORDS AND MUSIC: This time the cycle starts at the third section (demand) and when completed (trio) goes back to the beginning (shout), ending with the third section again. Words are slightly different and the orchestral texture is often simpler, softer and lower in tessitura. Aura tape fades.

3rd SONG OF MAGIC (The Song of the Tides, verse 3).
As before, but words changed to indicate that it is a fishing-net rather than a bird skull which is about to be uncovered.
   Aura tape recurs and gradually pitch falls an octave.

APOLLO TAPE: Word Command.

RESPONSE I: (variation of previous response)

# SEQUENCE 3   (Orpheus is killed by a thunderbolt)

Tide uncovers the fishing-net: events witnessed 'from behind'.

ACTION: Once again Orpheus and Aristaeus Puppets construct a huge destructible paper puppet of Orpheus which is destroyed by a thunderbolt.

SCENERY: As before, but rivers are now completely removed.

WORDS AND MUSIC: Second verses of Recitative of Teaching, Aria of Prophecy and Sentence of Religion. Music exactly as before.

# THE COMPOSER IN CONVERSATION

*THE FOLLOWING IS A résumé of conversations held in Lunegarde, Lot on 19 and 20 December 1983, when Birtwistle was composing his third opera, Yan Tan Tethera which BBC Television commissioned and have scheduled for production some time in late 1984. At that stage, including interruptions caused by the move to his new house, he had been working on it for about six months and was about three-quarters of the way through. Tony Harrison had provided him with the second and final draft of the libretto in April 1980, so there had been a fairly lengthy gestation period. Compared to The Mask of Orpheus it will be a modest affair lasting, probably, no longer than an hour. It is cast for four trebles (two sets of twins), soprano (Hannah), tenor (the Piper/the Ban'Un), two bass-baritones (Shepherd Alan and Caleb Raven), a chorus of twelve women and one man (Cheviot sheep/Wiltshire sheep) with an orchestra of six wind, percussion, harp and seven strings (minimum). Only one set is required, a landscape. Birtwistle hopes that in the studio the cameras will move in and around it. He stresses, however, that essentially the piece is intended for the theatre.*

*What's it about?*
It's a simple tale about numbers. Yan tan tethera means one two three, and it's the way shepherds used to count their sheep in the Pennines. When they reached twenty they'd transfer a pebble from one pocket to another and start again. It's based on a story I found in K. M. Briggs's *British Folk Tales*. The events take place in Wiltshire and concern a northern shepherd who has settled in

143

the Downs with a ram and ewe: 'I came from t'North with one ewe and one ram and I don't care much for this place where I am, but the ram tupped the ewe and she's likely to lamb...'. He and his sheep stand on one hill, while on another is a local shepherd with a large flock of Wiltshires. The point is that though the northern sheep multiply, the southern ones don't. As a consequence, the southern shepherd thinks it has to do with the way the northern shepherd counts, so he calls on the Bad'Un to help him counter the magic. We've called it a mechanical pastoral and it's really a peg on which to hang a very interesting theatrical device: as well as being very formal, everything that happens is done by counting. When Shepherd Alan says 'Yan tan tethera' the sheep multiply, the seasons change and so do the years—in ten pages I've gone through seven of them. The whole thing is like a big clock mechanism, like one of those intricate clocks you get in Bavaria.

I thought it was going to be an occasional piece, but it's turning out much bigger than I anticipated. It has things I've never done before and I'm really quite excited about it. Did you know that it was Stravinsky who divided Auden's text for *The Rake's Progress* into recitatives and arias? Auden wrote his libretto without the divisions. Well, I'm imposing something on Tony Harrison's libretto. Had I asked Tony to provide it for me, it wouldn't have worked; the result would be too formal in the wrong sense, too predictable.

At one level I'm doing what I always do. An analogy would be wandering through a town with squares, various squares, some more important than others, a town with roads on which you go round and round, in through one square out through another. You then come back again and approach from another angle, and so on. In other words, various parts of the piece get repeated. But in *Yan Tan Tethera* the repeats are not like ritornellos, they're not the same thing seen from a new perspective, they take context into account.

It's to do with what is background, what is foreground. In the section I'm composing at the moment the text is strophic. Hannah, the northern shepherd's wife, bewails the loss of her twins who have been ensnared by the Bad'Un. When she counts the years they've been missing, the sheep respond in dialect. This is the section in which we go rapidly through the years. For example: 'I grieve for my twins FOUR years gone away. Yan tan tethera methera. I grieve for my twins FIVE years gone away. Yan tan tethera methera pimp.' Now what I've done for the first time is this: on one level the music repeats, but on another there's a long—how can I describe it?—a long organic, fugue-like texture in the orchestra which goes right through the section then blossoms into a chorale when the counting reaches the magic number seven. So I have a strophic superstructure as foreground and an organic substructure as background which are independent, or largely independent, of each other.

You see, you can create a formal position before the event, an elaborate schemata, and that you can call your idea. That's what you're trying to express. You have a duty to that schemata, a duty to that initial idea. But in the process of composition you make contexts which are not necessarily concerned with it. Other things are thrown up which have a life of their own and are just as important. You now have a duty to two things. When writing *Tragoedia, Verses for Ensembles* or *Punch and Judy* I felt I had only one duty and that was to stick to the initial idea. Within that mould I made my jelly. Now two things are happening and it's interesting that one is concerned with the text, the other with the music.

In *The Mask of Orpheus*, as you point out, I invented a substructure which is not analagous with the text. There's a musical level and a dramatic level and they don't start coming together until the last act. But this was part of the formal, pre-compositional design and is completely artificial. In *Yan Tan Tethera* the substructure is more intuitive. Situations occur when the music creates a counterpoint to the drama in ways I have not predicted.

Let me give you another example. In the libretto Tony repeatedly refers to something he calls 'the music of the hill'. There are three references to it in the stage directions for the opening, for instance:

> Total darkness. We hear the 'music' of the hill, which is composed of voices (12 female, 1 male). Slowly we see

145

something like a sunrise but without the light. The hill rises slowly like a black sun over the horizon. We should feel it is actually a sunrise until half way over the horizon it stops, a round, unnatural looking hill, an ancient burial mound, such as one sees everywhere in the landscape of Wiltshire. From behind the round hill we should then see the 'real' sunrise, and the scene is slowly revealed as the traditional 'Arcadian' pastoral, green hill, bright blue sky, yellow sun. As the light increases 'the music of the hill' becomes less audible, goes 'underground' ... At the foot of the hill is seated Shepherd Alan with a Cheviot ram and ewe. If the hill is to be imagined as a painted flat, or a decorative clock-face background, then it should be painted summer on one side and winter on the other, and its turning should show the passage of the seasons in a stylized fashion, like the mechanism of an intricate clock. In the distance we should see another mound on which stands the motionless silhouette of Caleb Raven and his herd of horned Wiltshire sheep ... When the seasons change, and the hill (or hills) turn the only constant should be 'the music of the hill'.

What Tony wants, I think, is something ethereal, something simplistic to which you can return when an action has been completed. But I found it absolutely irritating. Every time I got back to this music I thought, 'Here goes the music of the hill again. Just go on repeating it.' But I couldn't, so I've utterly contradicted the idea. There is no music of the hill. Instead I've used those moments for instrumental music that's always different. Now, I hope, no one will say 'Ah, the music of the hill.' It's always different and it's always concerned with the context in which it's placed. I don't want to pick something up I've dropped some time back and slot it into a new context willy-nilly. The context of the moment is unique and must exert an influence, a strong influence.

In the past, if seven 'music of the hills' were needed and each had to last about a minute, I'd have composed a stretch of music lasting seven minutes, cut it into sections and provided each section with a beginning and an end. This is how I composed

*Verses for Ensembles*, probably the most extreme example of this way of proceeding. I know some people think it simplistic. It is, but at the time I had to do it like that. I had to have excessively bold orchestration and contrasting ensembles. I had to make a statement. At least it isn't a lie like *Medusa*. *Medusa*'s a piece with something stuck here, something stuck there without rhyme or reason. There's nothing in it which has the right to be placed next to a Bach chorale, least of all to be transformed into one. It's a lie, and I didn't see through my own lie; that's why I don't like it.

I could never write a piece like that again, never. But the new departures I've made in *Yan Tan Tethera* haven't arisen out of the blue, the seeds were planted some time back. They appear in the substructure of *The Mask of Orpheus*, and they're also in the *Clarinet Quintet* (58). In this I wanted to write some small postcard-sized statements, all using the same very simple format, like entries in a diary, perhaps. They were constructed from a pentatonic doodle I found interesting. I gave myself one condition: each had to be exactly as long as the paper I was using. It wasn't a question of writing until I came to the end of the sheet, then stopping; each had to fit the page exactly, each had to be complete. And for some reason, when I'd composed about eight of these pieces, which were like fragments except that they were through-composed because of the rule I'd imposed, I couldn't let them be, I had to join them together, I had to write links. But I couldn't leave the links alone either. As well as relating them to the statements I had to relate them to each other. As a result the piece became a long, continuous line and none of the original elements can be distinguished. Perhaps the changes in my music are due to changes within me. I don't know.

*You say these new events are happening intuitively, but in the past you've been sceptical about intuition?*

I don't think creative people think about their intuition. You take it for granted you're expressing yourself. It's a nineteenth-century, romantic idea that creative artists are people who are preoccupied with self-expression. What really preoccupies artists is simply how the hell you do it. It's not a question of having ideas, ideas are ten a penny. I've enough in my head to see me through four lifetimes. That's not the problem. The problem is how to make use of ideas, how to proliferate them, and this needs more than intuition.

First of all you need to have an idea of the world you want to create. For me, the worlds I most admire, the worlds I identify with, are those of artists such as Uccello, Piero della Francesca, Paul Klee. When I was young, Piero made a tremendous impact. Do you know a painting called *The Flagellation*? The lyricism, mystery and formalism it contains are qualities I've always wanted to emulate. The actual flagellation is taking place in the background on the left of the picture. There's a symmetry which is not a symmetry. In the foreground on the right are the figures of three men standing as if lost in their own worlds. But they're not puppets, they're genuinely human, and as far as information is concerned, they constitute the most important element in the picture. In fact the flagellation is not what the painting is about at all. The essence of the painting lies beyond its subject. It's about something else.

When I embarked on *Punch and Judy* and *The Mask of Orpheus* I knew the kinds of worlds I wanted to create long before I'd chosen the subjects. In the case of *Punch and Judy* I wanted a theatrical event that at one and the same time was very formal, a myth and English. The subject I eventually selected had the advantage of having a story everyone knew so that it wouldn't distract people from understanding what I was really trying to say.

When Tony Harrison and I got together for what eventually resulted in *Yan Tan Tethera* we didn't have an idea between us. So I said let's indulge our theatrical fantasies, let's find an interesting device, let's put masks on people, let's have fun. And that's how most of my pieces begin. I indulge my fantasies: I allow intuition to take over.

The piano chords which open *The Fields of Sorrow* and which also occur in such pieces as *The Triumph of Time* and ... *agm* ... were found when I was sitting at the piano trying to give octave Es depth and perspective. As you know I create centres of

148

gravity by giving one element in a complex statistical prominence. In a chord consisting of the five notes surrounding E to make let's say D sharp the centre of gravity all I do is include more D sharps in the chord than any of the other notes. The same applies to pulse for to my mind pulse and the octave are equated. In this particular instance a spread of Es gets disturbed by adjacencies so that you're not quite sure you're on E or not. I like that fuzziness.

But intuition only takes you so far. After that you need a method of working which enables you to manipulate the material. However, I've only once been able to explain my method and that was when my son Silas asked me what I did with all those numbers and I felt it my duty to tell him. It was some time ago and I've forgotten what I said but I couldn't do it again. I've certainly created a vocabulary for doing things but some items get thrown out, some forgotten. At the moment the working out of an idea seems very ephemeral. I've become acutely aware of the sanctity of the context. In any case it never seems to help me when composers talk about what they do. All that matters is that the composer has a responsibility to his material. But that's obvious.

What I can say is this: at the root of my music is ostinato, varied ostinato. Now if you have something which is to be varied you know that each time it occurs it must change. But the order in which it changes doesn't matter a damn. That can be left to chance. When I create these contrapuntal ostinatos, one piled on another, I feel like a dry-stone waller. You know that when the dry-stone wallers pick up a stone they always find a place for it in the wall. They never reject it. What I do is a bit like that. My material has been created by some chance operation, by random numbers most likely. I pick up the first thing that comes to hand and find the most suitable place for it. Having created a context I then generate more material and so the piece gradually gets bigger.

To change the analogy, I also feel like one of those medieval carvers Nicholas Pevsner discusses in those books he wrote for King Penguins: I carve the stone or the piece of wood to make the object I want, but there are elements in the material beyond

149

my control. So the essential nature of the stone or the wood remains inviolate. It has a life of its own.

I've noticed that when a group of actors walk on to a stage and stop the shape they'll make will be marvellous. But as soon as a stage director says 'Could you come over here', or 'Oh, I can't see him, will you stand there', or 'Could we have the leading man down front', it's ruined.

What I'm saying is best summed up by the work of Paul Klee. In the *Pedagogical Sketchbook* he's finding ways to proliferate his material, trying to make the sparks fly. It's full of the most marvellous ideas, but it's theory. If you then turn to the *Notebooks* and compare the theoretical sketch on one side of the page with the finished picture on the other you realize that the difference between them lies in the brush-stroke, the patina, which was neither contained in the theory nor present in the sketch. It's this which gives the finished picture its spontaneous quality, its magic.

In music, unfortunately, we don't have brush-strokes; we only have a pitch and a duration. So to compensate I use random numbers. These create the life of my music, the spontaneity. And I've always used them. At first I generated my own, but ever since *Chorales for Orchestra*, I think, I've used the computer-generated numbers my old school-friend Peter Lee gave me. I certainly used them in *Verses* for clarinet and piano. That's why you couldn't trace back to source the adjacencies in verse four. By the way I'm pleased you selected it for detailed discussion. It really is a microcosm of what I do. It's very formal, understated, fragmentary, it has repeats, it's through-composed and yet it doesn't quite add up. I'm very fond of it. You talk about things I wasn't conscious were in it, but that doesn't mean they're not true. If you've found them, they're relevant. A composer doesn't necessarily know what he's composed. He needs others to tell him.

There's another point about random numbers I'd like to mention. In using them I can extract a point of view which is not mine. Everything I've ever written is a multiple object. What is shown at any one time can only be a facet of it. I can never show its entirety. To give you a simple example. At the beginning of

*Yan Tan Tethera*, when the two shepherds are on their mounds, Shepherd Alan says, 'I wave; he never waves back.' Then the hills move and Caleb Raven says, 'He waves; I never wave back.' That's the same moment. Shepherd Alan's not still waving three minutes later. It's the same thing from the other person's point of view expressed in sequence rather than simultaneously.

What I find interesting are those situations where I create the multiple object but others select which facet is to be looked at. Take those ritornellos in *Cantata* or *Verses for Ensembles*. I provided the total object but gave the players and conductor fairly free reign as to what the line should be. They could select from the options I'd given them. Now that's like a random choice because it's not my choice. But when you listen to those ritornellos they always sound like the same thing. It doesn't matter what the players choose, it always sounds like a version of the same object. But that's only because of the number of players: five in *Cantata*, four in *Verses for Ensembles*. Were there additional players to cover more of the options the sound would be completely different. So in the end the crucial choice is mine. I've been able to distance myself from the object, given it, through the players, a degree of autonomy so that it has a life of its own, found a new perspective on it, but I've never lost control. That's the important thing.

*Nevertheless you tolerate mistakes—printing errors, for instance?*

No. No, I don't. The printing errors in such pieces as *Précis* are terrible. I don't tolerate them at all. When mistakes occur, such as the mistake in the flute part of *Refrains and Choruses* which you mention, it's the result of a memory lapse, my own memory lapse. I don't like inventing systems not generated from the moment that I actually require them. If I arrive at a context where a procedure is required, I will always invent or re-invent a procedure. I will never look back to see how I did it before. That would be too academic. I think that that's what's wrong with some of Messiaen's music. He finds a way of doing something and repeats it verbatim. So, apart from very rare exceptions, I either create something new or call on memory in order to make every situation unique. I know it's rather silly, but if I've turned the page and want to repeat something from the previous page I always do it from memory. I would never copy something out again from another page. That's where the so-called mistakes or errors come from.

*When you've completed Yan Tan Tethera what's the next piece?*

A little piece lasting thirteen minutes for the Polish Chamber Orchestra, a string piece that'll be given at the 1984 City of London Festival.

*What will be the routine? How will you start?*

Wasn't it Yeats who said start with anything—as soon as you have a context, anything. I would never formalize, never predict what the piece is going to be, because the one sacred thing is the context. As soon as I move (and it's Paul Klee again), as soon as I make a gesture and move to another there's a situation with ramifications. Things I would never have thought of in the first place appear. To these I have a duty. They are highly potent. From then the formalism starts showing itself. There's certainly no pre-composition.

*But you do know precisely its length?*

Yes, and it's called *Still Movement*. I know that. I'm hoping it's going to be a spin-off from the pastorals in *Yan Tan Tethera*. In the opera when the hills on which the two shepherds stand revolve, or when there's a movement from spring through winter to spring again, the accompanying pieces are pastorals. They're very short, but they'll be nice ideas for a little string work. And to create some kind of dramatic conflict, to create a protagonist and chorus, I'll divide the orchestra into two. But then once I sit down and start doing it, it might not be that. That's only the premise from which I'll start. What it will be when I've finished, I really can't say.

*And who are you writing for?*

Heavens! That's a difficult one. I think in the end I'm writing for myself. That's the only way I can hope to communicate with

152

people. Were I to think of an audience I'd probably think of the lowest common denominator. I don't want that. No, I do what I do as clearly as I can. That's all.

# CATALOGUE OF WORKS

1. *Refrains and Choruses* for wind quintet (flute, oboe, clarinet, horn and bassoon). In seven sections: through repetition, the refrain (the recurring element) becomes a predominant entity and so the chorus (the constant element) of the following section.
Completed New Year's Eve, 1957. Dedicated to Alexander Goehr.
First performed at 1959 Cheltenham Festival by Portia Wind Ensemble, Town Hall, Cheltenham, 11 July 1959.
Recorded (1966) by Danzi Wind Quintet on Philips SAL 3669.
U.E. 12931.

8 minutes

2. *Monody for Corpus Christi* for soprano, flute, horn and violin.
Text: the old English carol, 'The Faucon hath borne, my make away', and James, John and Robert Wedderburn's lullabye, 'O my deare hert young Jesu sweit'.
Composed 1959. Dedicated to Allen Lambert.
First performed by Dorothy Dorow and the New Music Ensemble, conducted by John Carewe, Recital Room, Royal Festival Hall, 5 April 1960.
U.E. 12928.

12 minutes

3. *Three Sonatas for Nine Instruments* Scheduled for performance by New Music Ensemble, conducted by John Carewe, at 1960 Aldeburgh Festival, Jubilee Hall, 17 June 1960; withdrawn after first rehearsal.
Unpublished and seemingly lost.

154

4. *Précis* for piano solo.           4 minutes
Composed Summer 1960. Dedicated to John Ogdon.
First performed by John Ogdon at Dartington Summer
School of Music, Dartington Hall, August 1960.
Recorded (1965) by John Ogdon on HMV ALP 2098 or
ASD 645.
U.E. 14158.
(Printed score—and recording—inaccurate; Maxwell
Davies owns the corrected copy.)

5. *The World is Discovered*         12 minutes
Six instrumental movements after Heinrich Isaac (1450-
1517) for two flutes, oboe, cor anglais, two clarinets (second
doubling basset horn or bass clarinet), two horns, two
bassoons, harp and guitar.
Three verses with three choruses; amplifies facets of *Der
Weld fundt, Tmeiskin uas iunch, Helogierons nous, Et ie boi
d'autant* and *Maudit soi* (Denkmäler der Tonkunst in
Österreich, Jahrg. XIV/I, band 28).
Commissioned by Tonus Musical Promotions (Anthony
Friese-Green).
Completed January 1961. Dedicated to Peter Maxwell
Davies.
First performed by Portia Wind Ensemble (with Marie
Goossens and John Williams), conducted by James Verity,
Recital Room, Royal Festival Hall, 6 March 1961.
U.E. 12937.

6. *Entr'actes* for flute, viola and harp.     *c.* 15 minutes
A cycle of five movements with coda: later the first part of
*Entr'actes and Sappho Fragments* (11).
Completed July 1962.
First performed by members of the Bournemouth
Symphony Orchestra, Cranborne Chase School, Wardour
Castle, Autumn 1962.
Not published separately.

7. *Chorales for Orchestra* (3 (all doubling piccolos), 3 (3rd     20 minutes
doubling cor anglais), 3 (2nd doubling E-flat clarinet, 3rd
doubling bass clarinet), 3 (3rd doubling contra)/4, 4, 3,
1/two harps, percussion (5 or 6 players)/strings).
Composed between December 1960 and October 1963.
First performed by New Philharmonia Orchestra,
conducted by Edward Downes, Royal Festival Hall, 14
February 1967.
U.E. 12955.

8. *Narration: A Description of the Passing of a Year* for *a cappella* chorus.     11 minutes

Text: sections 22 and 23 of the fourteenth-century romance, *Sir Gawain and the Green Knight*, translated by Brian Stone (Penguin Classics, 1959).
Composed October and November 1963.
First performed by John Alldis Choir, conducted by John Alldis, Wigmore Hall, 14 February 1964.
U.E. 14157.

9. *Music for Sleep* for children's voices, piano and percussion (at least three players). A lullabye for children under 11 to perform.     15 minutes

Commissioned by *Musical Times* and *Music in Education* (Novello and Co. Ltd) and published in their editions of March 1964. Composed November 1963. Dedicated 'to the boys and girls of my two schools: Knighton House, Port Regis'.
First performed by pupils of Knighton House and Port Regis Schools under the direction of the composer, Bryanston School, Winter 1963.

10. *Three Movements with Fanfares* for chamber orchestra (1 (doubling piccolo), 1, 1, 1 / 2, 2, 2, 0 / harp, timps (doubling percussion) strings).     14 minutes

Commissioned by the Worshipful Company of Musicians for the 1964 City of London festival.
First performed by English Chamber Orchestra, conducted by John Pritchard, The Guildhall, 8 July 1964.
U.E. 12989.

11. *Entr'actes and Sappho Fragments* for soprano, flute, oboe, violin, viola, harp and percussion.     25 minutes

Texts taken from *The Greek Anthology, with an English translation*, Harvard University Press, 1916-18.
Five entr'actes with coda, a connecting movement in which voice sings wordlessly, then five songs interspersed with new versions of the entr'actes and a second coda.
Completed Spring 1964.
First performed at 1964 Cheltenham Festival by Mary Thomas and Virtuoso Ensemble of London, conducted by John Carewe, Town Hall, Cheltenham, 11 July 1964.
U.E. 12948.

12. *Ring a Dumb Carillon* for soprano (doubling suspended cymbals), clarinet and percussion. Text: Christopher     12 minutes

Logue's 'On a matter of prophecy' from *Wand and Quadrant*, Collection Merlin (Olympia Press, 1953).
A dramatic scena in which the clarinet carries the monody.
Composed Winter 1964-5.
First performed by Noelle Barker, Alan Hacker and Christopher Seaman at an ICA concert, Arts Council, London, 19 March 1965.
Recorded by Mary Thomas, Alan Hacker and Barry Quinn on Mainstream MS 5001.
U.E. 14192.

13. *Carmen Paschale* Motet for SATB with organ obbligato.  **6 minutes**
Text (in Latin) by Sedulus Scottus (*c.* 850) in Helen Waddell's *Mediaeval Latin Lyrics*, Constable, 1929.
Commissioned by BBC Transcription Service for 1965 Aldeburgh Festival. Completed New Year's Day, 1965.
First performed by Purcell Singers, conducted by Imogen Holst, with Simon Preston, Aldeburgh Parish Church, 17 June 1965.
U.E. 12975.

14. *Tragoedia* for flute, oboe, clarinet, horn and bassoon  **15 minutes**
(all doubling claves), two violins, viola, cello and harp.
Based on the formal structures of Greek tragedy: Prologue—Parados—Episodion (Strophe, Anapaest, Antistrophe)—Stasimon—Episodion—Exodos.
Commissioned by the Melos Ensemble. Composed Spring 1965. Dedicated to Michael Tippett on his 60th birthday.
First performed by Melos Ensemble, conducted by Lawrence Foster, Wardour Castle Summer School of Music, 20 August 1965.
Recorded (1967) by Melos Ensemble, conducted by Lawrence Foster on HMV ASD 2333; reissued on Argo ZRG 759.
U.E. 14179.

15. *Verses* for clarinet and piano.  **6 minutes**
Composed Autumn 1965. Dedicated to Alan Hacker.
First performed by Alan Hacker and Stephen Pruslin, Architectural Association, Bedford Square, London, October 1965.
U.E. 14206.

16. *The Mark of the Goat* Dramatic cantata for actors,  **35 minutes**
singers, two choruses, three melody instruments, three players at one piano, large and small percussion ensemble.
Text by Alan Crang.

157

The action (in four scenes) involves the defiance of a military dictator by women anxious to give decent burial to a political martyr. Suitable for children between the ages of 11 and 13.

Commissioned by BBC Schools Programmes and first performed on sound radio during Spring Term 1966.
U.E. 14193.

17. *The Visions of Francesco Petrarca* Allegory for baritone, mime ensemble, chamber ensemble (flute, oboe, clarinet, horn, trumpet, trombone, two violins and cello) and school orchestra (1 (or recorder) 110 / 1111 / percussion (many players) / strings).
Text: Edmund Spenser's translation of seven sonnets by Petrarch (1304-74).
Six incidents of beautiful things destroyed by 'troublous fate' related by baritone with chamber ensemble; events gone through again in mime with school orchestra; all unite for final tableau.
Commissioned by 1966 York Festival. Composed between October 1965 and May 1966.
First performed in Church of St Michael-le-Belfrey, York, 15 June 1966, by Geoffrey Shaw, students of St John's College, York (mime), an amateur chamber ensemble, conducted by the composer, and the orchestra of Archbishop Holgate's Grammar School, York, conducted by Robin Black. The producer was David Henshaw, the designer Antony Denning.
U.E. 14176. Withdrawn for revision.

**65 minutes**

18. *Punch and Judy* a tragical comedy or comical tragedy in one act, for high soprano (Pretty Polly, later Witch), mezzo-soprano (Judy, later Fortune-Teller), high tenor (Lawyer), high baritone (Punch), low baritone (Choregos, later Jack Ketch), basso profondo (Doctor), and five mime dancers; on stage, a wind quintet (flute (doubling piccolo), oboe (doubling cor anglais and oboe d'amore), clarinet (doubling E-flat clarinet, bass clarinet and soprano saxophone), horn and bassoon (doubling contra); in the pit, trumpet, trombone, harp, percussion (2 players), 2 violins, viola, cello and double-bass.
Libretto by Stephen Pruslin.
Prologue, four scenes (each consisting of a melodrama and a quest for Pretty Poll) and epilogue.
Commissioned by English Opera Group. Composed between January 1966 and 8 January 1967. Dedicated to

**110 minutes**

158

'my pretty Poll'.
First performed by English Opera Group (Jenny Hill, Maureen Morelle, John Winfield, John Cameron, Geoffrey Chard and Wyndham Parfitt) conducted by David Atherton, Jubilee Hall, Aldeburgh, 8 June 1968. The producer was Anthony Besch, choreographer Alfred Rodrigues and designer Peter Rice.
Recorded (1980) by Phyllis Bryn-Julson, Jan De Gaetani, Philip Langridge, Stephen Roberts, David Wilson-Johnson and John Tomlinson with London Sinfonietta, conducted by David Atherton, on Decca, HEAD 24/25. U.E. 14191.

19. *Chorale from a Toy-Shop*                                    *2 minutes*
*First version*: for flute, oboe or clarinet, clarinet or cor anglais, horn or trombone, bassoon or tuba.
Commissioned by *Tempo* for Igor Stravinsky's 85th birthday and published in its 81st edition, Summer 1967. Composed April 1967.
First performed by Lancaster University Chamber Group, All Saints Church, Lewes, 28 March 1979.
*Second version:* for 2 trumpets, horn, trombone and tuba.      1-5 minutes
First performed by Philip Jones Brass Ensemble, Queen Elizabeth Hall, 19 May 1978.
U. E. 16046

20. *Monodrama* for soprano (Protagonist), speaker (Chore-      40 minutes
gos), flute (doubling piccolo and alto flute), clarinet (doubling A-flat, E-flat and bass clarinets), violin, cello and percussion (2 players).
Text by Stephen Pruslin.
Based on an early form of Greek tragedy in which a single actor takes on numerous dramatic functions.
Commissioned by Anglo-Austrian Music Society for the first concert of Pierrot Players. Completed April 1967. Dedicated to Peter Maxwell Davies.
First performed by Mary Thomas and Pierrot Players, conducted by the composer, Queen Elizabeth Hall, 30 May 1967.
Score withdrawn.

21. *Three Lessons in a Frame* for piano solo, 4 instruments    20 minutes
(flute (doubling piccolo), clarinet, violin, cello) and percussion.
Explores visual image of a mould and its copy. The first two lessons, for piano alone and instruments alone

159

respectively, are really the same work twice, except that whatever is implied but missing in one of them is to be found in its complement. In the third lesson the two interlock.

Commissioned by Macnaghten Concerts for 1967 Cheltenham Festival. Dedicated to Stephen Pruslin.

First performed by Stephen Pruslin and Pierrot Players, conducted by Peter Maxwell Davies. Town Hall, Cheltenham, 17 July 1967.

Score withdrawn.

22. *Nomos* for four amplified instruments (flute, clarinet,     15 minutes
horn and bassoon) and orchestra (4 (2nd, 3rd and 4th doubling piccolo), 3 (3rd doubling cor anglais), 3 (2nd doubling E-flat, 3rd doubling E-flat and bass clarinets), 3 (3rd doubling contra) / 4, 4, 3, 1 / harp, celeste, percussion (6 players) / 10 violas, 10 cellos, 8 double-basses.

Single movement in which the amplified instruments, as the 'law-givers', lay down a continuous *cantus firmus* that orders both micro- and macrostructure.

Commissioned by BBC for 1968 Promenade Concerts. Composed Winter 1967-8.

First performed by BBC Symphony Orchestra, conducted by Colin Davis, Royal Albert Hall, 23 August 1968.

U.E. 14671.

23. *Linoi*     10 minutes
*First version*: for clarinet in A (with extension down to C)     (all versions)
and piano.

Title implies 'a broken line'; single arch with piano playing pizzicato throughout.

Composed late Summer 1968.

First performed by Alan Hacker and Stephen Pruslin at an ICA concert, Purcell Room, 11 October 1968.

*Second Version*: the same with the addition of tape (Realization: Peter Zinovieff) and dancer.

First performed by Alan Hacker, Stephen Pruslin and Clover Roope, Queen Elizabeth Hall, 22 April 1969.

*Third Version*: for clarinet and piano with cello.

First performed at 1981 Huddersfield Contemporary Music Festival by Alan Hacker, Peter Hill and Jennifer Ward-Clarke, Huddersfield Polytechnic Music Hall, 19 November 1981.

U.E. 15313.

24. *Four Interludes for a Tragedy* for basset clarinet in A and     each about
tape (Realization: Peter Zinovieff). Reworkings of the     4 minutes

160

interludes in *Monodrama* (20); intended to frame the two halves of a concert.

Score prefaced with a quotation from Djuna Barnes's novel *Nightwood* (1936): 'With shocked protruding eyeballs, for which the tragic mouth seemed to pour forth tears.'

First performed by Alan Hacker, without tape, Conway Hall, London, 18 October 1968; with tape, Queen Elizabeth Hall, 10 February 1969.

Recorded (1977) by Alan Hacker on L'oiseau-lyre DSLO 17.

U.E. 16047.

25. *Verses for Ensembles* for woodwind quintet (piccolo doubling alto flute, oboe doubling cor anglais, clarinet doubling E-flat clarinet, clarinet doubling bass clarinet, bassoon doubling contra), brass quintet (two trumpets, horn, two trombones) and percussion (three players).    28 minutes

Commissioned by London Sinfonietta. Composed Winter 1968-9.

Dedicated to Bill Colleran (of Universal Edition).

First performed by London Sinfonietta, conducted by David Atherton, Queen Elizabeth Hall, 12 February 1969.

Recorded (1974) by London Sinfonietta, conducted by David Atherton, on Decca HEAD 7.

U.E. 15331.

26. *Some Petals from my Twickenham Herbarium* for piccolo, clarinet, viola, cello, piano and bells.    2½ minutes

Commissioned by Universal Edition to celebrate the 80th birthday of Dr Alfred A. Kalmus. Composed March 1969.

First performed by Pierrot Players, conducted by the composer, Queen Elizabeth Hall, 22 April 1969.

Recorded (1976) by a group of Spanish musicians, conducted by Cristobal Halffter on U.E. 15043 (ID 104).

27. *Down by the Greenwood Side* a dramatic pastoral for soprano (Mrs Green), actors (Father Christmas, St George, Bold Slasher, Dr Blood), mime (Jack Finney); flute (doubling piccolo and alto flute), clarinet (doubling E-flat and bass clarinets), bassoon (doubling contra), cornet, trombone, euphonium, percussion (one player), violin and cello.    40 minutes

Text by Michael Nyman based on the traditional English Mummers' Play and the ballad of the Cruel Mother.

One act divided into scenes devoted to Presenter, Combatants, Dispute, Lament, Cure and Quete, inters-

161

persed with various versions of the ballad.
Commissioned by Ian Hunter for the Brighton Festival
Society. Composed Winter 1968-9.
First performed in Festival Pavilion, West Pier, Brighton, 8
May 1969, by Jenny Hill and Music Theatre Ensemble,
conducted by David Atherton. The producer was John
Cox, the designer Antony Denning.
U.E. 15321.

28. *Cantata* for soprano, flute (doubling piccolo), clarinet     11 minutes
(doubling high-pitched B-flat clarinet), violin (doubling
viola), cello, piano (doubling celeste) and glockenspiel
(doubling small bongo).
Text by the composer taken from tombstone inscriptions
and translations from Sappho and *The Greek Anthology*.
Composed Spring 1969. Dedicated to 'Jill and Robin'
(Yapp).
First performed by Mary Thomas and Pierrot Players,
conducted by the composer, Purcell Room, 12 June 1969.
U.E. 15344.

29. *Ut Heremita Solus* An arrangement of the motet by      7 minutes
Ockeghem (*c.* 1425-95); for flute (doubling piccolo and alto
flute), clarinet (doubling bass clarinet), viola, cello, piano
and glockenspiel.
First performed by Pierrot Players, conducted by the
composer, Purcell Room, 12 June 1969.
U.E. 15366.

30. *Hoquetus David* An arrangement of the motet by        4 minutes
Machaut (*c.* 1300-77); for flute (doubling piccolo), clarinet
in C, violin, cello, glockenspiel and bells.
First performed by Pierrot Players, conducted by the
composer, Firth Hall, University of Sheffield, 22 October,
1969.
U.E. 15368.

31. *Medusa*                                                21 minutes
*First version*: for flute (doubling piccolo), clarinet (doubling
A-flat clarinet and soprano saxophone), viola, cello (all
amplified), piano (doubling celeste), percussion, two
electronic tapes (one synthesized sounds, the other an alto
saxophone distorted) and shozyg (an instrument invented
by Hugh Davies amplifying the sounds of small objects
inside a container).
Commissioned by BBC for an Invitation Concert.

162

Composed September 1969.

First performed by Pierrot Players with Peter Zinovieff (electronics), conducted by the composer, Firth Hall, University of Sheffield, 22 October 1969.
Score withdrawn.

*Second version*: the same except that viola doubles violin and shozyg is replaced by synthesizer.   50 minutes
Extended by parodies of Bach's Chorale Prelude on the Magnificat: *Meine Seele erhebt den Herren* and the Chorale *Wer nur den lieben Gott lässt walten.*
First performed by same artists, Queen Elizabeth Hall, 3 March 1970.

32. *Eight Lessons for Keyboards* Eight musical objects with   Variable
instructions on how they might be realized.
Durations variable.
First performed by Stephen Pruslin, doubling piano and celeste, Purcell Room, 13 January 1970, when he interspersed them between Beethoven's Bagatelles, Op. 119.
Not published.

33. *Signals* for clarinet and electronic sounds.   Tape lasts
The player, on hearing a signal on tape, chooses from five   45 minutes
possible sets of responses.
Commissioned by the Richard Demarco Gallery, Edinburgh.
First performed by Alan Hacker in the Demarco Gallery, August 1970.
Not published.

34. *Nenia: the Death of Orpheus* for soprano, three bass   17 minutes
clarinets (1st doubling B-flat clarinet), piano (doubling prepared piano) and crotales.
Text by Peter Zinovieff.
Dramatic scene in five sections.
Commissioned by Jane Manning. Composed Autumn 1970.
First performed by Jane Manning and Matrix (Alan Hacker, Ian Mitchell, Francis Christou, Paul Crossley and Tristan Fry) at a BBC Invitation Concert, Maida Vale Studios, London, 20 November 1970.
Recorded (1973) by Jane Manning and Matrix on Decca HEAD 7.
U.E. 15410.

35. *Dinah and Nick's Love Song* for three melody instruments and harp.
Commissioned by Dinah and Nick Wood and dedicated to them.
Composed Autumn 1970.
First public performance by Matrix at a BBC Invitation Concert, Firth Hall, University of Sheffield, 26 October 1972.
U.E. 16040.

5 minutes

36. *Meridian* for mezzo-soprano, horn, cello, two 3-part choirs of sopranos, 3 oboes (doubling cors anglais), 3 clarinets (doubling bass clarinets), 2 harps, piano and percussion (2 players).
Text: Christopher Logue's 'The image of love' from *Wand and Quadrant, Collection Merlin* (The Olympian Press, 1953), and lines from Sir Thomas Wyatt's 'Blame not, my lute' and 'My lute awake'.
Commissioned by the London Sinfonietta. Composed Winter 1970-71.
First performed by Yvonne Minton, Barry Tuckwell, Jennifer Ward-Clarke, members of London Sinfonietta Chorus and the London Sinfonietta, conducted by David Atherton, Queen Elizabeth Hall, 26 February 1971.
U.E. 15430.

30 minutes

37. *Prologue* for tenor, bassoon, horn, 2 trumpets, trombone, violin and double-bass.
Text: the opening of the Watchman's speech from *Agamemnon* by Aeschylus, translated by Philip Vellacott, Penguin, 1956.
Commissioned by 1971 English Bach Festival for Philip Langridge and London Sinfonietta. Composed early 1971. Dedicated 'to Michael and Aet' (Nyman) 'on the occasion of Molly'.
First performed by Philip Langridge and London Sinfonietta, conducted by the composer, English Bach Festival, 18 April 1971.
U.E. 15491.

8 minutes

38. *An Imaginary Landscape* for 4 trumpets, 4 horns, 3 trombones, tuba, 8 double-basses and percussion (four players).
A single movement built from five different sound-blocks.
Commissioned by BBC for 1971 ISCM Festival in London.
Composed between January and May 1971. Dedicated 'to the memory of my mother'.

17 minutes

164

First performed by BBC Symphony Orchestra, conducted
by Pierre Boulez, Royal Festival Hall, 2 June 1971.
U.E. 15474.

39. *The Fields of Sorrow* for 2 sopranos, chorus, 3 flutes,    9 minutes
3 cors anglais bass clarinets, 3 bassoons, horn, vibraphone
and 2 pianos.
Text by Decimus Ausonius (*c.* 310-95) contained in Helen
Waddell's *Mediaeval Latin Lyrics*, Constable, 1929.
Commissioned by Dartington Summer School of Music.
Composed July 1971, revised February 1972.
First performed by students at Dartington Summer
School, conducted by the composer, Dartington Hall, 7
August 1971.
Recorded (1974) by Jane Manning and London
Sinfonietta, conducted by David Atherton on Decca
HEAD 7.
U.E. 15462.

40. *Tombeau in Memoriam Igor Stravinsky* for flute, clarinet,    3 minutes
harp and string quartet.
Commissioned by *Tempo*. Composed September 1971.
First public performance by London Sinfonietta,
conducted by Elgar Howarth, St John's Smith Square, 17
June 1972.
U.E. 16045.

41. *Chronometer* for two asynchronous 4-track tapes.    24 minutes
Realized by Peter Zinovieff.
Composed Winter 1971-2.
First performed at a Redcliffe Concert, Queen Elizabeth
Hall, 24 April 1972.
Recorded (1975) on Argo ZRG 790 (two-track).

42. *Epilogue* for baritone, horn, 4 trombones and 6 tam-    7 minutes
tams (2 players).
Text: Shakespeare's 'Full fathom five' (*The Tempest*).
Commissioned by Globe Playhouse Trust for
Shakespeare's birthday.
Completed 15 April 1972.
First performed by Michael Rippon and London
Sinfonietta, conducted by the composer, Southwark
Cathedral, 23 April 1972.
U.E. 16056.

43. *The Triumph of Time* for orchestra (3 (3rd doubling    28 minutes
piccolo), 3 (2nd and 3rd doubling cors anglais), 3 (2nd and

3rd doubling bass clarinets), soprano sax, (amplified), 2
(2nd doubling contra), contra bassoon / 4, 4, 4, 2 / piano, 2
harps, percussion (5 players) / strings, at least 20 violins, 9
violas, 9 cellos and 9 double-basses).
Commissioned by the Royal Philharmonic Orchestra.
Composed between Summer 1971 and Spring 1972.
First performed by Royal Philharmonic Orchestra,
conducted by Lawrence Foster, Royal Festival Hall, 1
June 1972.
Recorded (1975) by BBC Symphony Orchestra,
conducted by Pierre Boulez on Argo ZRG 790.
U.E. 15518.

44. *La Plage: Eight Arias of Remembrance* for soprano,     14 minutes
3 clarinets, piano and marimba.
Text taken from *La Plage* by Alain Robbe-Grillet.
Commissioned by BBC for an Invitation Concert.
Composed Summer 1972.
First performed by Jane Manning and Matrix, Firth Hall,
University of Sheffield, 26 October 1972.
U.E. 15539.

45. *Grimethorpe Aria* for brass band (E-flat cornet, 8 B-flat     14 minutes
cornets, flugel horn, 3 E-flat horns, 3 trombones, 2
euphoniums, 2 B-flat baritones, 2 EEb-flat basses, 2 BB-flat
basses.
Score prefaced with quotation from Blake's *Jerusalem*
(Chapter 3, Plate 55, lines 57-8): 'Let the Indefinite be
explored, and let every Man be Judged by his own Works.'
Commissioned by Grimethorpe Colliery Band for 1973
Harrogate Festival. Composed between March and June
1973. Dedicated to Elgar Howarth and the Grimethorpe
Colliery Band.
First performed by Grimethorpe Colliery Band, conducted
by the composer, Royal Hall, Harrogate, 15 August 1973.
Recorded (1976) by Grimethorpe Colliery and Besses o' th'
Barn Band, conducted by Elgar Howarth on Decca
HEAD 14.
U.E. 15562.

46. *Chanson de Geste* for amplified sustaining instrument     10 minutes
and pre-recorded tape (Peter Zinovieff).
Related to *Grimethorpe Aria*. Contrasts 'a continuous
element and an intermittant, more percussive element'.
Commissioned by and dedicated to Fernando Grillo.
Composed May 1973.

First performed by Fernando Grillo (double-bass), Perugia, July 1973.
U.E. 15561.
Score withdrawn.

47. *Five Chorale Preludes* An arrangement of J. S. Bach's
*Durch Adam's Fall ist ganz verderbt, Wer nur den lieben Gott lässt
walten, Christus, der uns selig macht, Jesus, meine Zuversicht, Das
alte Jahr vergangen ist* for soprano, clarinet, basset horn and
bass clarinet.      18 minutes
First performed by Jane Manning and Matrix,
Roundhouse, London, 15 September 1975.
U.E. 15559.

48. *Melencolia I* for solo clarinet in A, harp and 2 string      *c.* 20 minutes
orchestras (each containing 15 violins, 6 violas, 6 cellos and
4 double-basses).
Title refers to the engraving by Dürer, 1502.
Commissioned for Musica Nova 1976 by the Scottish
National Orchestra Society. Completed July 1976.
Dedicated to the memory of Tony Wright (of Universal
Edition).
First performed by Alan Hacker and Scottish National
Orchestra conducted by Alexander Gibson, Bute Hall,
Glasgow University, 18 September 1976.
U.E. 16128.

49. *For O, for O, the Hobby-horse is Forgot* for six percus      27 minutes
sionists.
Title taken from Act III, scene 2 of *Hamlet*: 'Then there's
hope a great man's memory may outlive his life half a year;
but, by'r Lady, he must build churches, then, or else shall
he suffer not thinking on, with the hobby-horse, whose
epitaph is, "For O, for O, the hobby-horse is forgot."'
Commissioned by Les Percussions de Strasbourg.
Dedicated to Andrew Rosner. Composed Summer 1976.
First performed by Les Percussions de Strasbourg, Tokyo,
10 February 1978.
U.E. 16137.

50 *Silbury Air* for flute (doubling piccolo and alto flute),      18 minutes
oboe (doubling cor anglais), clarinet (doubling bass
clarinet), bassoon (doubling contra), trumpet, horn,
trombone, piano, harp, percussion (one player), 2 violins,
viola, cello and double-bass.
Score is prefaced by a Pulse Labyrinth.

Commissioned by The Koussevitzky Music Foundation in
The Library of Congress for the Chamber Music Society of
Lincoln Centre to honour the centenary of the birth of
Serge Koussevitzky. Completed 18 February 1977.
Dedicated to the memory of Serge and Natalie
Koussevitzky.
First performed by London Sinfonietta, conducted by
Elgar Howarth, Queen Elizabeth Hall, 9 March 1977.
U.E. 16141.

51. *Pulse Field (Frames, Pulses and Interruptions)* Ballet in
collaboration with Jaap Flier for 6 dancers and 9 musicians
(3 bass trombones, 2 amplified double-basses and
percussion (4 players)).

35 minutes

Title refers to way music and dance are built in small
frames and sections, related to a flexible pulse and
interrupted by relationships that develop between the
performers.
Commissioned by Ballet Rambert.
First performed by Ballet Rambert at 1977 Aldeburgh
Festival, Maltings, Snape, 25 June 1977. The designer was
Nadine Baylis.
U.E. 16146.

52. *Bow Down* Music theatre for 5 actors and 4 musicians
(bamboo flute, bamboo pipes, oboes, penny whistles and
percussion).

50 minutes

Text by Tony Harrison based upon various versions of the
ballad of the Two Sisters.
First performed by members of the National Theatre at
Cottesloe Theatre, 5 July, 1977. The director was Walter
Donohue, music director Dominic Muldowney, designer
Jennifer Carey, choreographer Judith Paris.
U.E. 16180.

53. *Carmen Arcadiae Mechanicae Perpetuum* for flute
(doubling piccolo), oboe, clarinet (doubling bass clarinet),
bassoon (doubling contra), trumpet, horn, trombone,
marimbaphone, piano or electric piano, 2 violins, viola,
cello and double-bass.

12 minutes

Six musical mechanisms juxtaposed many times without
any form of transition.
Commissioned by London Sinfonietta. Composed
Autumn 1977. Dedicated 'to my friends the London
Sinfonietta on the occasion of their tenth birthday'.
First performed by London Sinfonietta, conducted by the

168

composer, Queen Elizabeth Hall, 24 January 1978.
U.E. 16166.

54. *...agm...*                                                       35 minutes
Music for 16 voices (4 S, 4 A, 4 T, 4 B) and 3 instrumental
groups (high—2 flutes (doubling piccolos), 2 oboes,
clarinet, 2 trumpets, horn, 2 violins, viola; low—bass
clarinet, bassoon, contra, 2 trombones, tuba, 2 cellos,
double-bass; punctuating—piano, 2 harps, percussion (3
players)).
Text: the Fayum fragments of Sappho with translations by
Tony Harrison.
Commissioned by Ensemble InterContemporain.
Composed between December 1978 and March 1979.
Dedicated to Nicholas Snowman.
First performed by the John Alldis Choir and Ensemble
InterContemporain, conducted by Pierre Boulez, Théatre
de la Ville, Paris, 9 April 1979.
Recorded 11-12 June 1982 at IRCAM, Centre Georges
Pompidou, Paris, by the John Alldis Choir and the
Ensemble InterContemporain, conducted by Pierre
Boulez on Erato STU 71543.
U.E. 16245.

55. *Choral Fragments from ... agm...* for 16 voices.            17 minutes
An arrangement of the vocal parts of *...agm...*
First performed by John Alldis Choir, conducted by John
Alldis, Concert Hall, Broadcasting House, London, 5
April 1979.
Not published separately.

56. *Mercure—Poses Plastiques* An arrangement of Satie's     19 minutes
ballet for flute (doubling piccolo and alto flute), oboe
(doubling cor anglais), clarinet (doubling bass clarinet),
bassoon (doubling contra), trumpet, horn, trombone,
piano, percussion (1 player), 2 violins, viola, cello and
double-bass.
Completed Raasay, 12 February 1980.
First performed by London Sinfonietta, conducted by
Elgar Howarth, Queen Elizabeth Hall, 4 April 1980.
U.E. 17606.

57. *On the Sheer Threshold of the Night* Madrigal for 4 solo     16 minutes
voices (S A (counter-tenor) T B) and 12-part chorus.
Text: Boethius' *Stupet tergeminus novo* (*The Consolation of
Philosophy*) contained in Helen Waddell's *Mediaeval Latin
Lyrics*, Constable, 1929.

Score is headed by the inscription: 'In 524 Anicius Manlius Severinus Boethius, ex-consul and Roman senator, died by order of Theodoric under torture in the dungeon of Pavia in his forty-fifth year.'
Commissioned by Hessischer Rundfunk, Frankfurt. Composed 1980.
First performed at Hessischer Rundfunk, May 1980, by John Alldis Choir, conducted by John Alldis, who also gave the British premier at Bath Festival, St Andrew's Church, Mells (Somerset), 31 May 1981.
U.E. 16410.

58. *Clarinet Quintet* for clarinet, 2 violins, viola and cello.     22 minutes
Composed Raasay/Bagua di Lucca/ Raasay, Summer-Autumn 1980. Dedicated to Sir William Glock.
First performed at 1981 Huddersfield Contemporary Music Festival by Alan Hacker and The Music Party, St Paul's Hall, Huddersfield, 21 November 1981.
U.E. 17324.

59. *Pulse Sampler* for oboe and claves.     8 minutes
Composed Summer 1981.
First performed at 1981 Huddersfield Contemporary Music Festival by Melinda Maxwell and John Harrod, Huddersfield Polytechnic Music Hall, 20 November 1981.
U.E 16402.

60. *The Mask of Orpheus* A lyric tragedy in three acts; for 2 sopranos (The Oracle of the Dead (doubling Hecate) and First Woman), 3 mezzo-sopranos (Euridice singer and puppet (doubling Persephone) and Second Woman), contralto (Third Woman), 3 tenors (Aristaeus singer and puppet (doubling Charon) and First Priest), 2 high baritones (Orpheus singer and puppet (doubling Hades)), baritone (Second Priest), bass-baritone (The Caller), *basso-profundo* (Third Priest), mime troupe and 12-part chorus (in pit). Orchestra: 3 flutes (1st doubling piccolo, 2nd and 3rd piccolos and alto flutes), alto flute (doubling bass flute), 3 oboes (1st doubling oboe d'amore, 2nd and 3rd cors anglais), cor anglais (doubling bass oboe in C), 3 clarinets (1st doubling E flat, 2nd E flat and bass, 3rd bass clarinets), bass clarinet (doubling contra-bass clarinet), 3 soprano saxophones (doubling bamboo pipes, recorders and conches), 3 bassoons (2nd and 3rd doubling contra), contra-bassoon/4 trumpets, 4 horns, 6 trombones, 2 tubas/3 harps (all amplified), small electric harp, 7 string

170

metal harp, *Noh* harp, electric mandolin, electric guitar and bass guitar, organ, percussion (7 players)/Pre-recorded tapes.

Text by Peter Zinovieff.

Acts I and II composed between Autumn 1973 and Spring 1975, Act III between Autumn 1981 and Autumn 1983.

61. *Duets for Storab* for two flutes.　　　　　　　　6-7 minutes
1. Urlar
2. Stark Pastoral.
3. Fanfare with Birds.
4. White Pastoral.
5. From the Church of Lies.
6. Crumluath.
Composed Raasay, January 1983.
First performed by members of the Endymion Ensemble, Rosslyn Hill Chapel, London, 25 March 1984.

62. *Deowa* for soprano and clarinet.　　　　　　　　10 minutes
Based on the phonemes contained in the title.
Composed early 1983.
First performed by Jane Manning and Alan Hacker, Wigmore Hall, 29 March 1983.
U.E. 17664.

*Other Music*
(none published)
*Sad Song*: a modal piano piece composed *c.* 1971 for his　　2 minutes
eldest son, Adam.

*Untitled Piece* for Bill Colleran's 50th birthday, for flute,　　1½ minutes
clarinet, horn and bassoon.
Composed November 1979.

*The Offence*: music for Sidney Lumet's film (1973).

*Amadeus, As You Like It, Brand, The Cherry Orchard* (with Dominic Muldowney), *The Country Wife, The Double Dealer, Hamlet, Herod* (with Dominic Muldowney), *The Oresteia, Tamburlaine the Great, The Trojan War Will Not Take Place, Volpone*: music for productions at the National Theatre (1976-83).

*In Preparation**
1. *Yan Tan Tethera*: an opera for BBC TV (1984) based on a Northern folk tale.
2. *Suite from the Mask of Orpheus.*

171

3. *Still Movement* for the Polish Chamber Orchestra (City of London Festival, June 1984).

13 minutes

4. *Secret Theatre*: an instrumental piece for the London Sinfonietta (Queen Elizabeth Hall, 18 October 1984).
5. *Songs by Myself* for voice and chamber orchestra (Queen Elizabeth Hall, 18 October 1984).
6. A work for Paul Sacher's Zurich Chamber Orchestra.
7. A large-scale work for the BBC Symphony Orchestra (1986).

* This list compiled Autumn 1983.

# THE COMPOSER'S NOTES ON SOME OF HIS WORKS

*Refrains and Choruses* (1)
Its compositional scheme is simple, having five sections, each section consisting of two elements: a constant one called 'chorus', and a recurring one called 'refrain'. The refrain, through repetition, becomes a predominant entity, and so the chorus material of the following section. In the final section, the two roles become modified. The chorus, as a voice, becomes dimmer (shorter and less dense), and the refrain, which is the first announced as a five-note chord at its widest possible arrangement, becomes closer until it is finally sounded in its closest arrangement as a cluster.

*Monody for Corpus Christi* (2)
The first movement is a simple arch, whose main member is the vocal line (to which all other parts are embellishments and from which they may be said to stem). Its rise and descent are emphasized by the gradual addition of instruments from the beginning and their subtraction towards the end, and by the gradually increasing complexity of the instrumental episodes separating the couplets of the text.

This movement leads without a break into an instrumental fantasia 'quasi fanfara', in contrasting sections; this serves as a transition between the different levels of tension of the two movements for voice which precede and follow it.

The third movement follows without interruption and again the overall form is very simple. Each of the two stanzas of the text grows in intensity towards its end; in between them there is a brief instrumental episode ending with a flute cadenza.

*Tragoedia* (14)
The work is intended to bridge the gap between 'absolute music' and theatre music. It contains a specific drama, but this drama is purely musical. The title does not imply 'tragic' in the nineteenth-century sense. 'Tragoedia' literally means 'goat-dance', and the work is concerned with the ritual and formal

aspects of Greek tragedy rather than with the content of any specific play. This idea is present in the work on various levels. The instruments are divided into three groups: wind quintet, harp, and string quartet. The cello and horn, being the 'odd men out' of their respective groups, act as individual opponents within the conflict, while the harp acts as linking continuo. This instrumental organization is not a reference to Renaissance antiphony; it is simply a reflection on the level of instrumentation of the drama which is also expressed in the form of the work. The essence of the work's structure is symmetry—more specifically, bilateral symmetry in which concentric layers are grouped outward from a static central pillar.

The work opens with a Prologue that stands apart from this symmetry as an event 'outside the piece'. Here, the polarity of horn/harp/cello is exposed, as is the pervasive procedure of binding the texture together with repeated pedal tones.

The Parados brings us to the outermost shell of the symmetry. At first, winds and strings share the same violent material. When a totally contrasting idea suddenly enters, *dolce*, the choirs comment separately on it, winds first, then strings. At the close of the section, the groups rejoin.

The first Episodion is itself divided bilaterally into Strophe-Anapaest-Antistrophe. The outer sub-sections set the individual against the group, horn v. strings in the Antistrophe. The Anapaest places the two solo intruments together. Here, the flautist plays claves.

Later in the work, other wind players do likewise. The fact that the claves are *not* played by an independent percussion section is basic to the work's premise. This does not mean that the visual element is essential: the ambiguity created in a live performance by the joining of winds and claves *expresses* the work's theatrical nature, but does not *define* it.

Although the Episodion is symmetrically complete in the small, it is also part of a larger symmetry which is not yet complete. This is what impels the music forward across the central Stasimon and into the second Episodion. Symmetry may be seen retrospectively as a static phenomenon; but incomplete symmetry, that is, symmetry in process of being formed, is dynamic because it creates a structural need that eventually must be satisfied.

The prominence of the harp in the Stasimon marks the centre of instrumental and of formal symmetry. Around the harp, the choirs contribute to one static texture.

The second Episodian begins the return journey. It is a mirror image of the first only to the extent that it reverses the characters: 'peaceful-peaceful-violent' becomes 'violent-violent-peaceful'. Apart from this reversal, the internal content of the first Episodion is freely arranged, so that the horn-cello duet of Anapaest 1 now appears in Strophe 2. The tutti of Anapaest 2 have no precedent anywhere in Episodion 1. Furthermore, the repeated appearance here of the characteristic harp cadence of the Parados means that the second Episodion is commenting on an earlier section which is not its analogue in the symmetry. If Parados-Episodion-Stasimon-Episodion-Exodos is represented as A B C $B_2$ $A_2$, the $B_2$ is 'confused' with A. The non-literal symmetry that results from all these changes is crucial, since an exact mirror structure, even though motivated earlier in the work, would limit the form unnecessarily to one dimension as the work drew to its close.

In fact, it is precisely the extent to which $Episodion_2$ departs from $Episodion_1$ that allows the Exodos to ape the events of the Parados with only one or two minor variations. The work ends with the harp cadence which, having gained several connotations during the work, can function locally to conclude the Exodos, and in the large to close the whole structure.

*Tragoedia* deals with a number of ideas which have not appeared explicitly in my work since *Chorales for Orchestra*, and its music appears practically note for note in my opera *Punch and Judy*, for which it was a preliminary study.

## The Triumph of Time (43)

... the relationship of the music to Brueghel's *Triumph of Time*; the etching more as a reflection of methods used in earlier pieces than as a model directly to be represented in sound. (Musical ideas had already crystallized before I saw the picture.)
Reflections such as these:
in the foreground, the overall image of the procession: a freeze-frame, only a sample of an event already in motion: parts of the procession must already have gone by, others are surely to come: a procession made up of a (necessarily) linked chain of material objects which have no necessary connexion with each other...
in the background, recurrent procedures that are continuously there if only seasonally—the maypole, a weather-vane, the tides...
the position of the spectator identical with the composer's during the process of composition...

*Proposition:* a piece of music as the sum of musical objects, unrelated to each other, apart from one's decision to juxtapose them in space and time.

*Method:* to draw up a list of procedures which can be applied in different ways to different musical objects.

*A mode of change:* so that, for instance, where A is an element that is circumscribed and never changes, one descends through a sequence of potentially unlimited degrees of change to the musical object which is a permanent state of change.

175

*Two examples:*

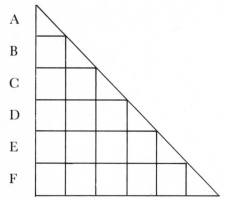

The cor anglais melody fulfils the role of A in the diagram as it repeats three times unchanged in the piece.

The second example, which would realize one of the middle positions, apparently never changes, until it explodes at the end of the piece, blossoming into a gigantic unison.

### Silbury Air (50)

Silbury Air is named after Silbury Hill, a prehistoric mound in Wiltshire, the biggest artifical mound in Europe, being 125 feet high and covering more than five acres. Its use and purpose, after centuries of speculation, still remain a mystery.

The music of the Air is not in any way meant to be a romantic reflection of the hill's enigmatic location—nor a parallel with any of its evident geometry. Seen from a distance the hill presents itself as an artificial but organic intruder of the landscape.

I have often alluded to my music of landscape presenting musical ideas through the juxtaposition and repetition of 'static blocks' or, preferable in my terminology, objects. These objects themselves being subjected to a vigorous invented logic via modes of juxtaposition, modes of repetition, modes of change.

The sum total of these processes being a compound artificial landscape or 'imaginary landscape', to use Paul Klee's title.

### Carmen Arcadiae Mechanicae Perpetuum (53)

The piece is by way of a homage to Paul Klee and the title is a title he could have invented. It consists of six mechanisms which are juxtaposed many times without any form of transition. The dynamics of the piece have a time-scale independent of that of the mechanisms, creating an independent dynamic life of their own. This process is also applied to the registers of the piece.

# SELECT BIBLIOGRAPHY

M. Bowen, 'Variation Forms', *Music and Musicians*. February, 1971, p. 34ff.

M. Bowen, 'Harrison Birtwistle', *British Music Now*, (Elek, 1975), p. 60ff.

M. Chanan, 'Birtwistle's Down by the Greenwood Side', *Tempo*, No. 89, 1969, p. 22ff.

E. Cowie, 'Birtwistle's Time Piece', *Music and Musicians*, June 1972, p. 22ff.

G. Crosse, 'Birtwistle's Punch and Judy', *Tempo*, No. 85, 1968, p. 24ff.

M. Hall, 'Birtwistle in Good Measure', *Contact*, No. 26, 1983, p. 34ff.

R. Henderson, 'Harrison Birtwistle', *Musical Times*, March 1964, p. 188ff.

M. Nyman, 'Two New Works by Birtwistle', *Tempo*, No. 88, 1969, p. 47ff.

M. Nyman, 'Mr Birtwistle in One', *Music and Musicians*, September 1969, p. 27ff.

M. Nyman, 'Harrison Birtwistle'. *London Magazine*, Vol. 11, No. 4, 1971, p.118ff.

H. Rees, 'Birtwistle's Medusa', *Tempo*, No. 92, 1970, p. 28ff.

R. Smalley, Birtwistle's Chorales, *Tempo*, No. 80, 1967, p. 25ff.

R. Smalley, Birtwistle's Nomos, *Tempo*, No. 86, 1968, p. 7ff.

S. Walsh, 'Birtwistle', *The New Grove* (Macmillan, 1980).

# INDEX OF WORKS

Numbers in brackets refer to the order in which works appear in the Catalogue on pp. 154-72.

179

# GENERAL INDEX

181